The
Bearded
Dragon

An Owner's Guide To

A HAPPY HEALTHY PET

Howell Book House

Hungry Minds, Inc.
Best-Selling Books • Digital Downloads • e-Books • Answer Networks •
e-Newsletters • Branded Web Sites • e-Learning
New York, NY • Cleveland, OH • Indianapolis, IN

Howell Book House

Hungry Minds, Inc.
909 Third Avenue
New York, NY 10022
www.hungryminds.com

For general information on Hungry Minds books in the U.S., please call our
Consumer Customer Service department at 800-762-2974. In Canada, please
call (800) 667-1115. For reseller information, including discounts and premium
sales, please call our Reseller Customer Service department at 800-434-3422.

Library of Congress Cataloging-in-Publication Data

Grenard, Steve.
The bearded dragon: an owner's guide to happy, healthy pet/by Steve
Grenard.
p.cm.
Includes bibliographical references
ISBN 0-87605-012-9
I. Bearded dragons (Reptiles)as pets. I. Title. II. Series.
SF459.L5G755 1999, 2001
639.3'95—dc21   98-47930
CIP

Manufactured in the United States of America

10 9 8 7 6 5 4

Series Director: Kira Sexton
Book Design: Michele Laseau
Cover Design: Michael Freeland
Photography Editor: Richard Fox
Illustration: Jeff Yesh
Photography:
    Front and back cover photos supplied by Bill Love
    All photography by Bill Love unless otherwise indicated
    Al Swanson: 36,60
Page creation by: Hungry Minds Indianapolis Production Department

Contents

part one

Welcome to the Wonderful Lizard of Oz

1 What Is the Lizard of Oz? 5

2 The Natural History of the Bearded Dragon 17

3 Anatomy and Physiology 28

part two

Your Pet Bearded Dragon

4 Why a Bearded Dragon? 36

5 Beardies: In and Out of Oz 39

6 Choosing a Pet Bearded Dragon 47

part three

Caring for Your Bearded Dragon

7 Housing Bearded Dragons 56

8 Feeding Bearded Dragons 72

9 Health Care for Bearded Dragons 83

10 Breeding Bearded Dragons 99

part four

Beyond the Basics

11 Bearded Dragons—An Australian Perspective 110

12 Resources 113

Welcome
to the
Wonderful

part one

Lizard of Oz

External Features of the Bearded Dragon

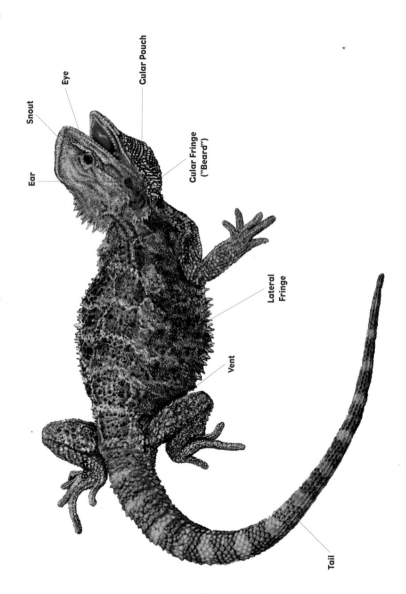

Snout

Ear

Eye

Cular Pouch

Cular Fringe ("Beard")

Lateral Fringe

Vent

Tail

chapter 1

What
Is the
Lizard of Oz?

According to legend, it all began with the bottom drawer of a filing cabinet. Lyman Frank Baum, some eight days short of his 42nd birthday, was sitting with his family and their children's friends on the evening of May 7, 1898, when the wonderful *Wizard of Oz* was invented. Baum was entertaining the children with a fairy tale about some fantastic characters when one little girl, beside herself with curiosity, asked "Oh please, Mr. Baum, where do they live?"

Baum, stuck for an answer, glanced around the room and caught a glimpse of a two drawer filing cabinet over in the corner. The top drawer was labeled A–N and the one, down under, O–Z. The rest is history. Oz was not only a magical place in Baum's fruitful imagination but, whether known to him or not, it was also the nickname Australians used to signify their country. Baum's Oz was truly a magical, wonderful place filled with many improbable creatures; and, remarkably, one could say the same thing about real world Australia. The truly amazing reptiles of Australia exist not somewhere over the rainbow but down under in Oz, so we could not resist nicknaming them the wonderful lizards of Oz!

Bearded Dragons are classified as members of the lizard family *Agamidae*. Agama lizards are known by a variety of common names including the chisel-toothed lizards, dragons, pricklenapes, and some have more terrifying but unjustified monikers such as Bloodsuckers and Thorny Devils *(Moloch horridus)* and are found virtually worldwide. Agamas are represented in Asia, Africa, the Middle East and, of course, in Australia. They have large mouths and a distinctive-shaped head. After looking at various kinds of agamas, you will soon be able to discern the family resemblance among them.

The Agama lizards include the rather unsightly Thorny Devil (Moloch horridus), *as well as our friend the beardie.*

The Bearded Dragons were originally assigned to the agamid genus *Amphibolurus,* a name derived from the Greek meaning "a tail that can be lashed this way and that" (two-directions). Clearly this name refers to a group of agamid lizards with long, thin whip-like tails. It soon became evident that the beardies were different from the rest of this genus and, in 1982, an Australian zoologist placed these unique lizards in their own genus called *Pogona*, which, in fact, means "bearded." By this time the question on everyone's mind is do these lizards really have beards? The answer is no . . . not in the conventional sense. No reptiles have hair, a growth restricted solely to mammals. Beardies do deserve their common name, however. They have a highly distensible throat (gular pouch), which is covered externally by filamentous floppy processes emanating from their scales that resemble a beard. Through muscular action they are able to erect these filaments in such a way so as to make the head and face look much bigger than it is. This is a defensive measure that beardies use to scare off predators, and it usually works. The end result to the human eye, however, is what can best be described as a beard! So the unbearded, tail-whipping dragons remained in the genus *Amphibolurus* but all the shorter tailed, tail-wagging, mostly "bearded" dragons were placed into the genus *Pogona*.

Another antipredator mechanism practice by many lizards is caudal autotomy or self-severing of the tail. This occurs within a vertebra along a specially developed fracture plane. Bearded Dragons may also lose their tails, but they do not have this fracture plane. Instead, their tails can snap off between vertebrae at their natural separation points.

The Types of Bearded Dragons

There are eight species of Bearded Dragon that are classified by scientists as follows:

FAMILY *Agamidae*
Genus Pogona
Species:

1. Bearded Dragon (Lizard). *Pogona barbata* (Cuvier, 1829).

2. Small-Scaled or Drysdale River Bearded Dragon. *Pogona microlepidota* (Glauert, 1952).

3. Western Bearded Dragon. *Pogona minima* (Loveridge, 1933).

4. Dwarf Bearded Dragon. *Pogona minor* (Sternfeld, 1919).

5. Mitchell's Northwest Bearded Dragon. *Pogona mitchelli* (Badham, 1976).

6. Nullabor Bearded Dragon. *Pogona nullabor* (Badham, 1976).

7. Inland or Central Bearded Dragon. *Pogona vitticeps* (Ahl, 1926).

8. Rankin's or Lawson's Bearded Dragon. *Pogona henrylawsoni* (Wells and Wellington, 1985). (Previously known as *P. rankini* and also known as *P. brevis*.)

The proper name (e.g., Cuvier, Sternfeld, Badham) that follows the scientific species name is that of the scientist who first identified, described and named the species. The year in which this occurred (e.g., 1829) follows their names. As you can see from the above list, all but one species *(P. barbata)* were officially described and identified in the 1900s. This is indicative of how little was known about these lizards until recently. The vast majority of reptiles were known to science in the eighteenth and nineteenth centuries.

All animals and plants are classified by special scientists called taxonomists, and all plants and animals are given a scientific name in a branch of taxonomy called nomenclature. Because they are technically a foreign language (derived from either Latin or Greek or the Latinization of other names), all scientific names are printed in italic type. All species have a generic name or genus that is capitalized, followed by a second or species name that begins with a lowercase letter. If a subspecies is referred to, it appears as the third name in the string. There are no known subspecies of the Bearded Dragons. All are members of the genus *Pogona*. The modern system of classifying plants and animals was invented by a Swedish botanist and physician, Carl von Linne, who Latinized his own name to *"Carolus Linnaeus."* However, the idea of giving all animals two- or three-part names, a system called "binomial or trinomial nomenclature" was devised 100 years before Linnaeus by Caspar Bauhin in Switzerland and John Ray in England.

If one is referring to an entire genus of animal or plant, it is customary to write the genus name followed by the designation "sp" for species or "ssp" for subspecies. This device is also used when the writer is not sure precisely which species or subspecies is being referred to. Thus, *Pogona* sp would be the correct scientific way of referring to all Bearded Dragons.

Pogona barbata

Pogona microlepidota

Pogona minima

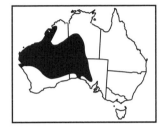

Pogona minor

Pogona mitchelli

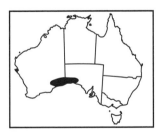

Pogona nullabor

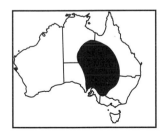

Pogona vitticeps

Pogona henrylawsoni

Almost all of Australia is home to at least one species of Bearded Dragon.

Bearded Dragons are found virtually all over Australia except the extreme north and far south. There is also fossil evidence that a species of this group was flourishing on Kangaroo Island some 10,000 to 16,000 years ago but is now extinct there. Although there is little that is certain about their evolutionary relationship, *P. barbata, P. henrylawsoni, P. minima* and the southwestern population of *P. minor* all share a yellow or orange mouth color.

Dragon Species
Eastern Bearded Dragon
(Pogona barbata)

The scientific name of this species, *"barbata,"* traces its origin to the word *barber;* the tie-in is obvious. It is the first member of this group of lizards described by scientists. Early Australians also called it the "Jew" Lizard because, evidently, the few Jews they had ever seen were sporting beards as well. It was not, in the slightest way, ever considered a slur or a name based on religious or racial prejudice. This species is one of the largest and heaviest of the Bearded Dragon clan, with early records of animals growing to 1 foot, 8.5 inches in total length, about 1 foot of which is the tail. Specimens nearing 2 feet have also been recorded. The Eastern Bearded Dragon is occasionally available in the pet trade in North America from captive-bred colonies.

In the wild, this lizard is found in eastern and southeastern Australia, but not on the Cape York Peninsula, Queensland or on Tasmania. It is semiarboreal, preferring to perch on low-lying branches, bushes and rocky outcrops, which are known as "tors" down under. It can frequently be seen perched on the tops of fence posts as well. It does well in a variety of different habitats, ranging from seasonally wet coastal forests to arid, inland scrublands. This species was originally named *Amphibolurus barbatus*. It is considered semiarboreal and feeds on a variety of flowers and tender leaves, and is frequently also observed basking on roads, a risky way to obtain belly heat.

DRYSDALE RIVER BEARDED DRAGON
(Pogona microlepidota)

This lizard is also known as the Small-Scaled Bearded Dragon (*microlepidota* is Latin for "small-scaled"). This is a relatively newly discovered species, first described to science in 1952. At the time of this writing, this species is not available anywhere in the world outside of Australia. This lizard is found mainly within an area comprising the Drysdale River National Park in the northernmost corner of Western Australia and other areas nearby. It is thus unlikely that overseas hobbyists will ever have the opportunity of working with this species. It is found in open woodland where a type of grass known as spinifex grows, as well as other low-lying ground shrubbery.

On occasion, Eastern Bearded Dragons are found in the pet trade.

WESTERN BEARDED DRAGON
(Pogona minima)

The Western Bearded Dragon is found over a vast swath of southwestern Australia in a variety of habitats, ranging from coastal sand dunes to heavily forested areas. Its range is from southwestern Australia far into the arid interior. It is semiarboreal and in the wild it perches and basks on fallen trees and rocks. Between October and February, it produces one or possibly two clutches of eggs, numbering from five to fifteen per clutch. During this time this species is found basking on roads and a great many get run over.

Some of these dragons may be available overseas as a result of previous smuggling efforts. Western beardies reach a maximum length of about 20 inches.

DWARF BEARDED DRAGON
(Pogona minor)

The Dwarf Bearded Dragon is also found in western Australia. However, it is a smaller species than its Western cousin, reaching a maximum body length of about 8 to 10 inches. Its range is from the central coast of Western Australia through central Australia and South Australia to the Eyre Peninsula.

MITCHELL'S BEARDED DRAGON
(Pogona mitchelli)

Mitchell's Bearded Dragon is found in northwestern Australia and is generally not available in the pet trade. Some scientists consider it a subspecies of *Pogona minor.* It is a small species, reaching a maximum body length of about 8 inches. Its range is from the lower Northern Territory to northwestern Western Australia, and it is found in dry woodlands and scrubland.

NULLABOR BEARDED DRAGON
(Pogona nullabor)

This lizard is found in the south central/southwest of Australia, principally on the Nullabor Plain in South and Western Australia. On the coast, it is found on steep cliffs and near caves. It differs from *Pogona barbata* by the presence of white bands across the back and tail, which may give it some desirability among breeders. The Nullabor Bearded Dragon reaches a maximum body length of about 8 to 10 inches.

INLAND OR CENTRAL BEARDED DRAGON
(Pogona vitticeps)

The Inland or Central Bearded Dragon is one of the most common species of Bearded Dragon, both in

Australia as well as in overseas collections. This species is the one you would be most likely to find sold by breeders, pet shops or at swap meets. The majority of this book on the care, keeping and breeding of Bearded Dragons refers to this species. The Inland beardie is widely distributed throughout the noncoastal areas of the eastern states through the eastern half of south Australia and north to southeastern Northern Territory.

It is found in a wide range of habitats, from dry forests and scrublands to the sandy deserts of the interior. It is semiarboreal and perches on roadside fence posts and hills, fallen timber or trees. It dines on vegetable matter, preferring soft leaves and flowers when available. It is also a voracious insect predator and will quickly consume large numbers of crickets or other live insect foods placed in its enclosure.

A long, large and heavy-bodied race of these lizards is being bred in Germany and they have earned themselves the nickname "German Giants."

The beard on Lawson's Dragon could be characterized as a five o'clock shadow.

LAWSON'S DRAGON
(Pogona Henrylawsoni)

Henry Lawson's Dragon is also known by two other common names: Rankin's Dragon and Black-Soil Dragon. It differs from all other members of the genus *Pogona* in one distinctive way: It is almost clean-shaven! Lawson's Dragon has practically no "beard," so it cannot

Welcome to
the Wonderful
Lizard of Oz

properly be called a Bearded Dragon, although it is similar to beardies in every other respect.

Henry Lawson's Bearded Dragon was first described to science in 1985 by Wells and Wellington, although many Australian herpetologists were previously aware of its existence. The name *"henrylawsoni"* took many years to become formally accepted, with rivaling scientists petitioning the International Commission on Zoological Nomenclature to suppress all new names proposed by Wells and Wellington. The petition was rejected, and the commission ruled that each new name would be reviewed on a case-by-case basis, based on the usual rules of priority. Thus, even though these authors were accused by others of "taxonomic vandalism," their proposed name for the species was ruled as official. Later names proposed for the species, namely *Pogona brevis* and *Pogona rankini,* were rejected. Before naming this species after Henry Lawson, Wells and Wellington wanted to name it after Alan Greer, a well-known Australian herpetologist, but Greer asked that he not be given this honor. Confusion reigned for many years after these events and accordingly, *Pogona henrylawsoni* can still be found on dealer/breeder advertisements and price lists incorrectly called *Pogona brevis* and *Pogona rankini.* There is more to this story, including personality conflicts and accusations that Wells and Wellington published an insufficient or extremely brief description of their lizard. At one point, the museum specimen they used mysteriously disappeared,

WHO IS HENRY LAWSON AND WHY DOES A BEARDED DRAGON BEAR HIS NAME?

Henry Lawson (1867–1922) is a famous Australian poet. The scientists Wells and Wellington, in naming this Bearded Dragon after him, decided it was high time Lawson was recognized with an Australian lizard of his own. No, Lawson didn't have a beard, but he did have a mustache. These Australian herpetologists also named species after corrupt politicians, a less than fitting honor for a reputable reptile . . . and they once even tried naming a reptile after Darth Vader! In the rules of scientific nomenclature, anyone who publishes a description of a species that has never been described before in writing can essentially name it after whatever or whomever they please. Aussie herpetologist Ray Hoser once named a new species after his dog, and the well-known Australian snake expert Richard Shine has been known to publish articles under the pseudonym: "Cooper Shine" (which happens to be his dog's name). In fact, newly described species are frequently named after dogs, because dogs often figure prominently in the animal's discovery.

then later resurfaced. In 1995, herpetologist Glen Shea published a photograph of the allegedly missing museum specimen complete with its authenticating museum tag and serial number.

The Henry Lawson's Dragon is found throughout the black-soil plains of central Queensland and has also been observed on similar terrain in nearby border areas of the Northern Territory. To escape predation in the wild, this lizard has been seen scuttling quickly into and between cracks in the soil. A known predator is the venomous Collett's Snake *(Pseudechis colletti)*. Unfortunately there are very few breeding stocks of Lawson's Dragon in the U.S., and they may be related. If so, this could ultimately make for a poor genetic outcome in future breeding attempts. These small stocks originated in Germany in 1984 and were probably derived from smuggled-out specimens of this (at the time) unnamed species. Because it is impossible to legally get any fresh stock from Australia, this species may have a poor outlook as far as the hobbyist is concerned. Several Henry Lawson's Bearded Dragon breeders in the U.S. have not, however, had any problems with their purebred stock.

Some breeders are mating Lawson's Dragons (top) with Inland Dragons (bottom). The majority of the hybrids fall somewhere between the two in size.

To confound matters even more, Henry Lawson's dragons may hybridize with *P. vitticeps,* both in the wild and deliberately (as well as inadvertently), in captivity. The results of such cross-matings are amusingly called "vittikins." Breeders of Lawson's

Dragons are very much opposed to cross-breeding them with Inland Bearded Dragons and argue that there is no reason to do so. Some of the offspring look like Inlands, and others look like Lawson's. In the size department, they fall midway between Lawson's smaller length (averaging 10 inches, including the tail) and the Inland beardie's greater length. According to one Henry Lawson's breeder, Jon Klarsfeld, such cross-breeding will destroy the Henry Lawson's Dragon gene pool, and buyers of Bearded Dragons will never really know what species they are getting. This type of cross-breeding is not the same as back-crossing animals of the same species for color or pattern or other fanciful reasons.

Henry Lawson's and Inland Dragons are different genetically, and cross-breeding can be disastrous for a species.

Body size, head shape, color, tail length and the extent of the beard growth are all altered in such hybrid crosses. Overall hybrids are larger than Lawson's but smaller than Inland beardies, with total lengths averaging 13 to 15 inches.

Purebred Lawson's Dragons are well suited for hobbyists with a lack of space for larger species. Breeders advise they have successfully mated and bred pairs in a 20-gallon aquarium, while larger species, such as the Inland Dragon, do best in a 125-gallon, 6-foot-long aquarium enclosure.

A NINTH SPECIES?

To add greater confusion to the mystery of Henry Lawson's Bearded Dragon, some Australian herpetologists believe that the specimens in the U.S. (which they have never examined) may be an as yet unnamed ninth species of Bearded Dragon. In theory, at least, *P. henrylawsoni* is known only from the black-soil areas of Queensland. Is the similar specimen from bordering northwest Australia a different species or merely a range extension of Lawson's dragon?

The Natural
History
of the
Bearded Dragon

Oz is truly the land of the lizard…
with its torrid, wide open inland
deserts (five of them in fact), all
of which support an amazing
abundance of lizard life, beardies
included.

When looking at an animal's behavior, one must consider its
natural history: temperature reg-
ulation, feeding behaviors and
diet, courtship, mating and reproduction, as well as defense
against and escape from predators. Understanding how these
behaviors work in the wild helps
hobbyists successfully maintain such animals in captivity. And on occasion, the converse is true: Observations made in captivity help
unravel mysteries that field biologists could never solve.

Temperature Regulation

Understanding how Bearded Dragons regulate body temperature is an essential part of keeping them well-fed, healthy and in tip-top condition. Like all other reptiles, beardies obtain heat from and throw off heat to their surroundings. Poikilothermy and homeothermy are two of the key terms used to describe how animals monitor their own body temperature. Animals that maintain fairly constant body temperatures or body temperatures within a narrow range (such as humans, whose normal body temperature fluctuates slightly between 97° and 99°F) are known as homeotherms; organisms with widely varying temperatures over time are known as poikilotherms. These two types of temperature regulators mesh with a second set of terms: ectothermy and endothermy. Ectotherms obtain heat from their surrounding environment, while endotherms produce heat internally. All reptiles are ectotherms. Notably, some scientists theorize that prehistoric dinosaurs were not ectotherms, and recent research indicates that some sea turtles maintain warmer core temperatures than the water in which they live.

Bearded Dragons inhabit the deserts of Australia.

Birds and mammals, including humans, are endotherms. Birds and mammals are also homeotherms. Remarkably, under some circumstances reptiles may also achieve a high degree of homeothermy—through their behavior, they can maintain a fairly constant body temperature (even though they are dependent on their environment for ensuring this). Bearded Dragons actually regulate their body temperatures carefully during certain times of the day by behavioral means, thereby rendering themselves homeotherms, or at least as "partial" homeotherms. What's more, beardies maintain body temperatures every bit as high as that of a bird or mammal.

Given the proper conditions in captivity or their normal Australian climates in the wild, beardies are anything but cold-blooded, a misleading term often used by some to describe reptile body temperature. Agamid lizards are prevalent in the world's deserts, and Australia is no exception. Ectothermy allows them to become metabolically inactive when food supplies are scarce. Beardies, in particular, are "low-energy" animals. A day's food supply for a rodent can last a beardie for several days or a week. Beardies do not expend much energy in search of food, as they are equally content eating vegetable matter as well as insect prey; they do not run very far or work very hard in pursuit of either type of foodstuff. If they find some tender leaves or flowers to eat, they can hang around such a location for hours, eating what they will when they wish.

Unlike many reptiles, beardies are active in the daytime, even during the hottest parts of the day, and are comfortable with temperatures well into the 90s. Because they obtain their body heat from the sun, they are also known as heliotherms. And because they are constantly moving in and out of the sun to regulate their temperature, they are called "shuttling heliotherms." At night they get heat not from the sun but from the ground beneath them that baked all day in the sun and is now suffused with heat. Thus, at the height of the noonday sun, their core temperatures may be around 92°F; at night they may drop, but not very much. An interesting parallel is found in endothermic human hospital patients whose body temperature is checked during the day and at night. During the day, human body temperatures may range from 98° to 99°F, but at night they drop to around 97°F.

It is important to understand that while beardies can withstand fairly high temperatures (into the 90s, as noted above), just a few degrees more can be fatal. Once

> **TA-TA LIZARDS—
> ANOTHER BEARDIE
> NICKNAME**
>
> The Bearded Dragon's deliberate rotation or waving of the foreleg that looks like arm waving is referred to by scientists as circumduction. This behavior has also earned beardies the nickname "ta-ta lizards," after the British colloquial expression meaning "so long" or "good-bye."

their environment reaches these high temperatures, keepers must be careful not to allow them to creep higher. To make sure this doesn't happen, it is okay to keep Bearded Dragons at maximum temperatures of around 85°F, giving them a sort of buffer zone at the high end.

TEMPERATURES DURING THE DAY AND NIGHT

When beardies emerge from their nighttime hiding places, their skin color is darkened, an adaptation designed to absorb heat rather than deflect it. As they warm up, their color lightens. Their first order of business in the morning is to move directly into a basking

spot, turning their backs to the sun with their spiny sides expanded to increase the surface area for heat absorption. Their color, shape and the way they orient themselves toward the sun all serve to optimize absorption of the sun's rays. They often choose a basking site that is a poor thermal conductor, such as wood or foliage, so that they won't lose heat to their underlying surface. In captivity, they will stand on their two hind legs, pressed against their plastic hiding spots or a piece of driftwood in their enclosure with their backs toward the light. They then might move to a branch and lay across it.

A Bearded Dragon that is gaping is too hot! Move it to a cool area immediately!

If you observe them carefully during the day, you will see them constantly shifting their position, sometimes imperceptibly, in order to gain more or less heat. As the day wears on and the environmental temperatures increase, beardies must take care to avoid becoming too hot. As previously indicated, the difference between the optimal temperature and too hot may be just a few degrees. To prevent overheating, beardies become very light in color, (light tan bordering on off-white). This helps to deflect heat. They will now orient themselves by placing their heads toward the sun, which minimizes the amount of body surface area available for heat absorption. They may also seek shelter under a shrub, bush or piece of timber, or climb into a tree, seeking shelter under its foliage.

As a last resort, when too warm, they will open their mouths (gaping) as if to pant in an effort to dissipate heat, much in the way a dog does. Scientists who have observed this behavior believe that when this happens, the lizard is one step away from being "cooked." It is important to remember this when you set up your beardie's captive environment. If your beardie takes to gaping or panting, it is too hot! Take appropriate action to correct this situation at once: Shut off basking lights and lower thermostats or heating pad temperatures. If necessary, move the animal to an unheated enclosure until panting stops. In extreme emergencies, take the lizard by hand and move it to a cool spot—in front of a fan or near an air-conditioning unit—until the gaping stops. Do not, however, put it in the freezer.

Eastern Bearded Dragons have been found hibernating during the hot Australian winters.

Hibernation

In Australia, activity patterns of Bearded Dragons are clearly dictated by ambient temperatures. On cooler days, active beardies will bask until they reach ideal temperatures, at which time they move about, mostly foraging for food. If body temperatures drop, they stop what they are doing and warm up again by resuming their basking behavior.

However, according to Australian field scientists, at higher temperatures beardies may seek shelter during the hottest days or during the hottest time of the day. It has been noted that no beardies were seen on several days of hot weather (100°F) in South Australia, but on the following cooler day, when the temperature was in the 40° to 50°F range, a Bearded Dragon was observed abroad, crossing a road. In 1970, Australian herpetologist Richard Wells was the first to describe what was true hibernation in a Bearded Dragon, and this has been confirmed many times over in the Sydney area, a cooler part of the Bearded Dragon's range. Ray Hoser, searching for reptiles to the southwest of Sydney with an associate, lifted a large slab of sandstone revealing a large, "sleeping" *Pogana barbata*. The slab of rock was well embedded and the lizard had dug a lengthy burrow to travel to where it was found resting. It was a sunny midwinter's day, and the locale was sheltered by bushes. Hoser says the lizard was in a torpid or inactive state, which means that it would be difficult to rouse, and was clearly hibernating. In other reptiles, captive breeders artificially hibernate both sexes prior to mating and breeding attempts, but this has not been described as a necessity in Bearded Dragons and it is difficult to say whether it would be a beneficial factor in breeding captive beardies.

WHEN IN ROME

If you have an opportunity to travel to Australia and to chat with the Aboriginal people, be aware that they refer to Bearded Dragons as "Mantalyarrpa" or "Japantarra." Herein, we will stick with Bearded Dragons or beardies.

Predator and Prey in the Wild

Bearded Dragons inhabit many areas where food resources may be scarce (arid scrublands), so they can't afford to be picky eaters—and they aren't. Beardies are omnivores, which means that they relish both animal and vegetable matter and subsist on either or a combination of both. Some of their desert- or plains-dwelling lizard relatives, such as American Horned Lizards (*Phrynosoma* sp) and the Australian Thorny Devil *(Moloch horridus)*, are dietary specialists. These species thrive principally on ants, doubtlessly available in vast quantities within their habitats. Because Bearded Dragons consume large quantities of either vegetable or insect matter, as available, they must have large stomachs to handle the load. Their appetites are accommodated by their tank-like body form (shared also with Thorny Devils and Horned Lizards), but this decreases the ability of the lizard to run and escape from predators. As a result, natural selection favored a spiny body form and the expandable "beard" as antipredator mechanisms rather than the sleek, long, torpedo-like body of other lizards capable of absconding at great speeds.

Beardies active in the daylight and spending prolonged periods in the open foraging on vegetation or the occasional insect passerby clearly are at increased risk of being preyed upon. Their beards, their spiny bodies and their sandy coloration cause them to be somewhat "invisible" against the substrate, and together serve to protect them against predation.

Beardies also show an unusual reluctance to move, even when directly threatened by a predator. This works to their advantage, as movement tips off predators as to their exact location and negates the ability of their protective coloration and contour to keep them concealed. This laid-back nature is one of their more endearing traits when handled as captive pets. They can be approached, picked up and kept perched on a human hand or arm for prolonged periods and they hardly flinch. It is not exactly fair, therefore, to characterize beardies as "tame" or especially calm. This is, in reality, their standard modus operandi.

Bearded Dragons will eat almost anything that could be considered food. In contrast, their cousins, the American Horned Lizards, subsist almost entirely on a diet of ants (Phyrnosoma platyrhinos).

If, on the other hand, a predator in the wild confronts a beardie at close range, the lizard will respond by blowing out its fake whiskers, flattening its body close to the ground and opening its mouth in a color-flashing gape. If all this doesn't work and it is actually attacked, a beardie will fight back. Beardies are truly the "gentlemen" (and "ladies") of the lizard world. First

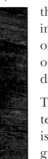

they try camouflage and "freezing," then bluffing (displaying of beard and gaping) and they only fight as a last resort in self-defense.

The camouflage and "freezing" technique of predator evasion is particularly important to the gravid ("expecting") female. Bearded dragons produce rela-

If it can't hide from a predator, a beardie will try to scare it off by displaying its beard and gaping.

tively large clutches of eggs, as often as two or three times a year. I knew of one female Inland Bearded Dragon that produced fifty-six eggs in one year in two separate clutches. Such a high number of eggs, representing perhaps as much as one-third of the total body mass, is undoubtedly a direct consequence of this lizard's robust body form. Sleek, fast-moving lizards, such as Anoles and Geckos, produce between one and two pea-sized eggs per clutch. But a beardie weighed down by twenty-five or more eggs (each about one-half the size of a Ping-Pong ball) cannot be expected to move that speedily. As a consequence, it is obvious that gravid female beardies rely almost entirely upon freezing and camouflage (rather than beard display) to fool enemies.

Beardie Interactions

After studying your Bearded Dragon in its captive home, you may soon become aware that it follows your every move visually. If food or a lizard in an adjoining cage comes into its range of sight, your beardie will become very attentive. Beardies and other agamids use their sight more than any other sense. This is because they are diurnal or daytime-active. They work out in the open, and so must be able to spot predators or food at great distances. Because adult Bearded Dragons have subtle sexual differences among males and females that are visually discernible, beardies also use their vision to detect potential mates. Social behavior involves a number of changes in arm or leg position, body shape, color and even color patterns. The head is bobbed up and down when mating occurs, and the throat may be distended and the body raised, with the animal elevating itself off the ground. Beardies also compress or depress their sides.

WAVING

Social interactions among Bearded Dragons consist of a unique set of movements that can only be construed as visual signals: Beardies resting on three legs will raise one of their front arms and, in a circular motion, slowly wave it about as if they were waving hello or good-bye to a friend on the street! It is not clear whether this is a greeting, a sign of submission or some sort of secret signal indicating to another lizard that it is a friend, not a foe. It is surmised that the first humans in Australia, the Aborigines, who were present as long as 40,000 years ago, picked up this arm waving trait by observing Bearded Dragons engaged in such behavior. It is also conceivable that the entire human repertoire of arm waving, or to signal hello and good-bye as a friendly action, was based on such early observations of these animals. The uncanny resemblance of this Bearded Dragon behavior to human arm waving is so remarkable that you would have to see it firsthand to believe it. Although I have witnessed this behavior in isolated beardies, it is even more prevalent when females come into visual range of males, as well as when one beardie sights another one (even in the next cage) regardless of sex. I have also observed it in large dragons that were evidently signaling to babies in adjoining enclosures—making it unlikely that this is purely an act of submission. The waving repertoire, therefore, probably has multiple functions, just as it does in humans.

One researcher has theorized that both tail waving and arm waving are related behaviors designed to attract a predator's attention as a sort of come-on. Bearded Dragons remain stock-still when arm waving, with eyes fixed firmly ahead of them. The behavior allegedly distracts the predator's attention away from the lizard itself, that then, as the predator gets close, bolts off rapidly. This explanation is flawed to the extent that it doesn't account for the behavior when a predator is not present. Moreover, it runs counter to the Bearded Dragon ploy of remaining completely still when approached by a predator, almost in a trance-like or frozen position, known scientifically as thanatosis (meaning "behaving like dead"). We know it better as "playing possum" or "playing dead." It just is not very likely that a Bearded Dragon will wave to a potential predator, saying in effect "Hey, I am over here. Come and get me if you can."

THE BEARDED DRAGON'S BIOLOGICAL CLOCK

Bearded dragons have a small, light-sensitive "third eye," also known as the pineal eye. The pineal eye is located between their eyes and beneath the parietal scale on the top of their head. This organ serves as a meter to detect solar radiation. Sensory input thus received triggers the release or inhibition of hormones, such as melatonin and prolactin, that control the daily cycle of activity, or circadian rhythm. This organ is, in effect, the lizard's biological clock. Not all reptiles have this organ. It is absent in crocodilians, several families of lizards, snakes and turtles; no bird or mammal has such an organ either, at least not one that functions in exactly this way.

Courtship and Mating Behaviors

In adult dragons, males and females can be readily distinguished. Males have a darkened throat pouch, giving their beard a more startling appearance than that of the female. Most agamids have pale pink tongues and throat linings, but a few species of Bearded Dragons have variations in this coloration. Henry Lawson's Dragon has a bright orange throat; the Eastern Bearded Dragon species and Inland Bearded Dragon have a yellowish throat. The reason(s) for these differences are not certain, but some believe that they assist in visual and/or sexual recognition. Male Bearded Dragons also have larger and better-developed pre-anal and femoral pores than the females, but these might not be a helpful visual cue unless you are looking at a male and female at the same time. Observations made on breeding groups reveal that, in general, males are slightly larger than females of the same age. If viewed simultaneously, one would note that males have larger, wider heads than females. The tails of male beardies are wider at the base and taper more gradually than that of females.

Captive-bred beardies in the U.S. lay their eggs from as early as February through the end of June. Throughout the spring months in North America, some beardies have been observed laying two or three clutches of eggs, producing up to eighty eggs during one season. (See chapter 10 for information on breeding your own pets.)

Sometime between 1 and 2 years of age, beardies reach sexual maturity. When a male and female are placed together, there is head bobbing, beard spreading and arm waving. During mating, the male latches onto and holds down the female by the nape of the neck. All Bearded Dragons are egg layers. It is interesting to note that in their native Australia, mating and breeding occurs in the Australian spring and summer months, September through March. However, dragons bred outdoors in the United States adapt to the reversal of seasons here quite nicely. Dragons kept indoors breed without regard to seasons.

The tail of a male Bearded Dragon (top) is wider at the base than that of a female (bottom).

chapter 3

Anatomy
and
Physiology

Body Shape

Bearded Dragons are four-legged, spine-covered lizards that are more or less disk- or tank-shaped, with a rounded body that lies close to the ground. They appear, in general body shape, more or less similar to the much smaller American Horned Lizards (also known as "horned toads"), although these lizards are not agamids but members of the family *Iguanaidae*. Both however, are well adapted to arid, desert-like conditions and both are found in a variety of dry habitats, ranging from desert to plains or scrublands, as well as forested areas. Their sandy coloration and blotchy patterns afford them excellent camouflage against their background. Those that live in red, sandy areas develop a reddish-coloration that improves their ability to conceal themselves.

Limbs

Bearded Dragons have four robust legs with five clawed toes on each foot. The claws are relatively soft and handlers are rarely, if ever, scratched by them. The front claws are used to obtain purchase on the tops of such basking objects as fence poles and tree trunks. The rear toes "dig in" to the objects so that the dragon does not fall off.

The female of the species uses her clawed feet to excavate a nest to lay her eggs. Mating behavior and reproduction in wild beardies has been documented by many, including early Australian herpetologist Kinghorn as long ago as 1931. More recently, the burrowing behavior of egg-laying beardies has been described when a *Pogona barbata* female was observed laying her eggs. According to reports, the female digs her nest by scooping out a hole long enough to bury herself in. She deposits her eggs and then emerges, carefully covering the entrance over before she departs.

Tail

All Bearded Dragons have a moderate-size tail that widens greatly toward the base. Unlike most other lizards, they do not practice true caudal autotomy (self-severing of the tail) to escape predators, nor do they have fracture planes in their tail vertebrae that would enable them to do this. They can, however, lose a part of their tail by having it bitten off, either by another Bearded Dragon or by a predator. If this happens, the remaining tail will heal up.

Spontaneous loss of a beardie's tail might occur between vertebrae as opposed to fracture planes within the bony process itself. Nineteenth-century Australian zoologists wrote that beardies would use their tails in a whipping motion to defend themselves. However, it is likely that this belief is not highly accurate. Beardies are not known to actively strike human handlers with their tails (at least mine never have). If tail whipping were a common defense, one would expect to see it used when handled.

Circulatory System

Like most reptiles, Bearded Dragons have three-chambered hearts. Their anatomy also enables them to change the pattern of blood flow within the head and body to help them control their temperature. When they first emerge into the daylight in the morning, they divert blood to large sinuses in the head. This heats up the dragon's brain and sensory organs first, paving the way to maximum functioning early in the day. When they bask, back facing the sun, their dorsal blood vessels dilate and their heart rate increases, which also helps speed up transfer of heat throughout the body.

Digestive System

The digestive system of Bearded Dragons begins with the oral cavity and teeth. Unlike many herbivorous reptiles, beardies chew their food using their teeth, releasing nutrients from within, thereby aiding in the digestion of vegetable matter. Food is swallowed and transmitted to the stomach via a relatively short esophagus.

In the stomach and the intestines that follow, the food is more thoroughly digested and is subject to microbial degradation or fermentation, a specialized type of digestion employed by animals that consume significant amounts of vegetable matter, including those that do so exclusively. Unlike herbivorous mammals (for example, horses, cows and rabbits), reptiles do not suckle or maintain close contact with their young following birth. Accordingly, newborn Bearded Dragons must obtain the bacteria necessary to help ferment and digest their food by ingesting fecally contaminated bits of soil. In captivity, therefore, newborn dragons should be started on a diet of small insects (pinhead crickets or fruit flies) until they have built up sufficient numbers of this kind of bacteria in order to obtain nutritional benefit from a vegetarian diet.

Bearded Dragons are indiscriminate feeders of vegetable matter and will eat leaves and fruits as well as bits of whole raw vegetable matter such as carrots. You can demonstrate the unique way Bearded Dragons chew their food by offering them a baby carrot or small piece of a larger carrot and watch them chew and pulverize it for swallowing and digestion. Beardies also eat flowers, such as yellow dandelions, and seem attracted to bright colors when feeding.

The intestinal tract terminates in an all-purpose cavity known as the cloaca. It terminates with an anal portal through which excrement or waste products are discharged to the environment. The cloaca is used not only for storage and ejection of fecal and urinary waste, but also for sexual intercourse and passage of eggs in reproduction.

Genito-Urinary System

The reproductive system of beardies is similar to that of all other lizards. It consists of paired, internally suspended gonads (ovaries in females, testes in males). Female ovaries communicate with the cloaca via oviducts, testes with a specialized intromittent organ known as a hemipenes, which is located inside the cloaca but which can be averted outward to accomplish true, internal fertilization of the female's eggs during mating.

Urinary wastes are processed by paired kidneys and empty into the cloaca for excretion by the ureters. As discussed earlier, beardies often go for long periods of time without water and often obtain what little water they can from their food. Thus, they must be able to conserve fluids. In order to rid themselves of urinary wastes while maintaining fluids, beardies and other reptiles with a similar problem excrete a "dry" urine, which appears as a chalky, white powdery substance consisting largely of the nitrogenous waste product known as uric acid. Whereas ammonia and urea are soluble in water, uric acid is not. When the liquid urine enters the bladder or the cloaca, water is reabsorbed. This process in reptiles permits the excretion of nitrogenous waste products with little or no fluid wasted in the process. This material, along with fecal wastes, is emptied to the outside via the cloaca.

Skin

The skin of Bearded Dragons is rough, warty or leathery. It contains many soft "spines" that make them somewhat unpalatable to larger predators. Their skin bumps are useful in obtaining water, living as they do in areas where rain or standing fresh water is scarce to nonexistent. When rain does occur, it washes through the dragon's scales and pours down onto its snout. Dragons have been observed standing in the rain, their bodies widely spread and pointed toward the rainfall. They lower their heads below body level and as the rain runs onto their snout they lick it off or catch it with their tongues. When water is not available, they conserve what they have by producing a concentrated semisolid urine, reabsorbing the watery part into their bodies. *Note:* As a desert species, they survive well in the absence of rainfall or drinking water, but captives should be sprayed lightly several times a week. Beardies also obtain water from their food, and their vegetable meals can be easily sprayed down with water to aid in this purpose (see chapter 8 for more information on providing food and water for your beardies).

The rough skin of Bearded Dragons has many soft "spines" that diminish their appeal to predators.

Senses

Bearded Dragons have Jacobson's organs in the roofs of their mouths. This organ, also found in snakes as well as in other lizards, functions like a cross between the senses of taste and smell. Unlike snakes and Monitor Lizards, however, beardies rarely use tongue flicking to check out the palatability or suitability of a plant or bug as a food item. They seem to rely almost entirely on their visual senses in this regard (because snakes have very poor vision, they depend on the chemical clues they pick up by tongue flicking). Beardies' eyes are mounted laterally on the sides of their head, thereby providing them little or no binocular vision; yet they can detect food, enemies or mates at distances of 100 feet. There are apparently no detailed studies concerning their ability to see colors. I have observed, however, that they can evidently discern certain colors and select items of food based on their coloration. In particular, they appear to see reds and yellows well, the colors of flowers that are a favorite food. Experiments performed on captive beardies indicate that they have excellent hearing; standing alert at loud or unusual noises. When they hold their bodies close to the ground, they can also detect ground vibrations, a sense that gives them

warning of large predators in the vicinity. Nonetheless, this ability does not seem to extend to pavement—when absorbing heat from roadways, a significant percentage of beardies get run over.

By holding their bodies close to the ground, beardies sense lurking predators.

Teeth

Although beardies resemble horned lizards in their body shape, it is their difference in dentition that sets them apart. Iguanids have their teeth set in small indentations on the inner sides of their jaw bones, an arrangement referred to as pleurodonty. Agamids, on the other hand, have all but their front teeth fused to the sides of their jaws, a condition known as acrodonty. The teeth of pleurodont iguanids fall out and grow back in at regular intervals, whereas agamids replace only their front, pleuordont teeth.

The two kinds of teeth seen in beardies and other agamids accommodate the wide diversity of their diets. The replaceable, pleurodont teeth are cone-shaped or pointed, whereas the more rearward permanent or acrodont teeth are compressed or chisel-shaped. The front teeth are useful for grasping and piercing, while the rear teeth are better suited to cutting and slicing, being especially adept at manipulating plant matter.

Your
Pet

part two

Bearded Dragon

chapter 4

Why
a Bearded
Dragon?

After nearly forty years' experience with moderate- to large-size lizards, I have to admit that beardies are absolutely the number one, most amazing lizard within this group. Although their coloration is not as spectacular as some lizards, and they rarely grow much beyond 2 feet in length, they make up for these "flaws" with many endearing traits and qualities. Let's look at the extra-neat things about the lizard of Oz.

Size

Beardies don't get very large. Two feet is a nice size, and they are comfortable at that size in a 30- or 55-gallon tank. If you want a bigger lizard, or think that a 2-foot animal is more than you want to manage, then beardies are not for you.

Feeding

Bearded Dragons eat both animal and vegetable matter. They can even be tricked into eating pellet food that is formulated just for them with the right combination of vitamins and minerals. Few reptiles are as easy to feed as Bearded Dragons, and even those who don't care to watch reptiles eat mice or bugs rarely mind having a beardie nearby.

Handling

When picked up and handled (gently), beardies don't scratch, bite, fight or try to whip you with their tails. They just act mellow and hope for the best. There is no other reptile that comes as close to being "naturally tame" as a beardie. None. By sitting calmly in your hand, they are merely manifesting their usual antipredator behavior, which is to freeze stock-still when they sense danger. For a beardie, being picked up by a "giant" human is danger. This makes beardies a relatively safe pet for children as there is little or no fear that the lizard will bite. However, if handled roughly or hurt in any way, all bets are off—beardies will defend themselves.

Because beardies tend to "freeze" when picked up, they can be gently handled. But they are delicate, and must be handled with care.

Appeal

Bearded Dragons have a number of anthropomorphic traits (human-like qualities) that make them all the more irresistible. Their attentiveness is unusual in a lizard, and they have the bizarre habit of waving one of their front arms in a circular motion—which absolutely flips people out the first time they see it. If you gave them a rag they could wipe down their enclosure!

Daylight Lizard

Beardies are active in the daytime just like (most) people so you can feed them, study them and handle them during daylight hours. Nocturnal lizards, such as nearly all the Gecko species, cannot be observed as readily except with special red or night-light bulbs.

Heat

You can provide Bearded Dragons with heat from an ordinary incandescent bulb turned on during the day and off at night. While they like to warm up to around 90°F in the daytime, their cage temperature can drop at night into the 70s. (See chapter 7 for more information on proper temperatures.)

Politically Correct

The entire pet market for these animals is met from captive breeding operations, so no beardies have to be removed from their natural environment to sustain such trade. Of course, it is illegal to export any kind of animal from Australia (even pest species), but their ease of breeding removes any financial incentive would-be beardie smugglers might have.

Thus, beardies stand out as an environmentally sound, politically correct and noncontroversial reptile-pet.

DRAGON GOES HOLLYWOOD

The attraction of beardies has reached to the stars. According to *PetLife* (Nov./Dec. 1998), Leonardo DiCaprio keeps a Bearded Dragon named Blizz.

Safe

Although random studies of reptiles in general indicate more than 90 percent carry salmonella, a germ that can be passed to humans, to date no Bearded Dragons have been implicated in human cases of the disease. This does not mean that beardies are not capable of getting and spreading this germ, so obey the rules in preventing zoonotic infection listed in the health care section of this book.

chapter 5

Beardies:
In and Out
of Oz

Australia is an island continent in the eastern half of
the southern hemisphere.
Its name derives from the
Latin word *australis,* meaning "southern." Bearded
Dragons are not naturally
found anywhere else on
earth. Australia is the
smallest continent on the
planet, measuring just under 3 million square miles, and it contains
vast tracts of desert, scrub and rocky terrain, as well as many salt
lakes. It is divided into six states and two territories. These are
Western Australia in the west, Northern Territory in the north,
Queensland to the east, New South Wales to the southeast, South
Australia in the south and Victoria in the southernmost eastern corner. An offshore island to the south, separated from Australia proper
by the Bass Strait, is the State of Tasmania. The Australian Capital
Territory (ACT) is the smallest political subdivision, just 939 square

Your Pet
Bearded Dragon

miles and is home to Australia's capital, Canberra. It is also in the southeast.

Australia is home to many unusual reptiles and amphibians, most seen nowhere else in the world. These include some of the world's most toxic venomous snakes and such oddities as the Frilled Dragon and Bearded Dragons. Other unique animals found in Oz are the primitive mammals known as the Duck-billed Platypus and Spiny Echnida, a host of marsupials, such as Kangaroos and Wallabies, and the famed teddy-like Koala Bear (which is not a bear at all but another type of marsupial).

Australian Wildlife Crises

Australia has had its share of ecological disasters. Nearly all of these problems were engineered by arriving Europeans in the nineteenth and early twentieth centuries, and nearly all involved the introduction of exotic plants or animals. These include a feral population of camels (brought there by well-intentioned settlers who felt they could be used to traverse Oz's vast deserts), feral cats and dogs and a plague of nonnative rabbits that eat most

Introduction of the Marine Toad to Australia has resulted in ecological havoc. The toads consume insects that are the natural fodder for other animals and kill their predators due to their toxic secretions.

types of vegetation in their path. A type of large toad, known down under as the Cane Toad (also known as the Giant Tropical or Marine Toad, *Bufo marinus*), was introduced to eat sugar cane beetles. Instead, the toad has reproduced unchecked in the millions and eats not only insects but outcompetes and eats other Australian wildlife that was not its intended target. Moreover, native animals (including reptiles) eat the toads and, as they have no immunity to the toad's toxic secretions, die.

Oz Prohibits Exports

Various Australian states started passing restrictive laws prohibiting the import or export of any plant or animal life. The prohibition became national law in the early 1960s, and since then it has been legally impossible to collect, keep or export any Australian wildlife without a permit. Export permits are extremely difficult to obtain. Rather than targeting individual endangered or threatened species, the Australian government felt it was simpler to enact a broad-sweeping and total ban. The law certainly simplified things administratively, but has caused great difficulties for hobbyists and scientists. It also sent the animal trade underground and encouraged smuggling and official corruption when officers were paid to look the other way (or were even involved in illegal animal deals themselves).

Although some species are extremely common (including many species of Bearded Dragon), they, too, are included in the ban. Critics of Australia's wildlife laws point out that by driving traders underground, critically endangered species (as well as common species) escape detection when being illegally collected and traded (or exported). In

---

THE TRAGEDY OF SMUGGLING

When animals are smuggled, they are often subjected to inhumane and crowded conditions. They may be trussed up for days or even weeks without food or water as part of legal shipments of canned goods or dry goods. Birds are tied up and their beaks taped shut so they will keep quiet. Smuggled turtles are taped around and stacked like books in crates barely big enough to contain them.

Another ploy is to smuggle out eggs instead of the animals themselves. Eggs need precise conditions of temperature and humidity to thrive. Such conditions in a smuggling operation are impossible to provide and most perish before ever hatching. But few get through by random luck so the smuggler can get his "payday."

To fight wildlife smuggling, do not buy such animals when offered.

---

the end, the illegal activity hurts the endangered species while protecting others that don't need protection. Moreover, because trading in rare and endangered species is more profitable to the smugglers, it is these species that are the prime targets of illegal export.

It is rumored that some "relief" from these onerous regulations may be forthcoming in a government plan to establish breeding colonies of selected species that are particularly popular worldwide. These animals could then be exported—to the ultimate benefit of the country and its export trade. If this does occur, Bearded Dragons are apt to be one of the first species selected for this purpose.

A precedent for such a program exists in the current existence of government-supported breeding farms for the common Green Iguana in Central America. The iguanas are being bred for food and leather as well as to support the pet trade worldwide. Such captive breeding operations remove the incentive to collect these animals from the wild and protect them in their natural habitat. Wild-collected reptiles are less likely to be as healthy or as well-acclimated as captive-bred and raised specimens. If a captive breeder charges a few dollars more for a healthy, nurtured specimen as opposed to a wild-collected animal, the consumer gets his money worth. It is hoped that one day all (or most) trade in wild-collected animals will cease and that trade in such animals will rely principally on their artificial propagation.

Governments of some Central American countries have deterred smuggling of Green Iguanas by supporting captive breeding operations.

How the Bearded Dragon Left Oz

In view of Australia's restrictive policies on the export of any wildlife, the question arises . . . how did Bearded Dragons find themselves in North America, Europe, Japan and elsewhere? Clicking their heels and chanting "there's no place like home" clearly was not effective.

Obviously, beardies, along with many other Aussie herps, such as the popular Frilled Dragon and a wide assortment of snakes, were smuggled out of Australia.

According to Ray Hoser, the author of two books detailing the illegal export of Australian animals, most Bearded Dragons were smuggled out of the country between 1974 and 1990. These were either stolen from licensed keepers in the country and/or seized by government wildlife officials in New South Wales. Hoser states that the animals were transported through Southeastern Asia and then on to Europe, Japan and North America, where they obtained legal status after being "laundered" outside of Australia. These animals formed the "founder stock" of what is seen outside Australia today.

Obviously, the large number of these animals that appeared in Europe, the U.S. and Japan from the mid-'70s to early '90s indicate that a good deal of smuggling took place that escaped detection. Authorities have documented a number of routes and methods used by smugglers to get reptiles and birds (and their eggs), out of Australia illegally.

There are some totally absurd stories that allegedly account for the existence of such animals outside of the Australia. One of the most common statements made by criminals is that the animal in question did not come from Australia at all, but from nearby Papua New Guinea (PNG). This is a half-truth, as PNG served as a common transit route for smugglers, as did New Zealand,

SMUGGLING STORIES

In his book *Smuggled: The Underground Trade in Australia's Wildlife*, Ray Hoser details the case of John Nichols from a press report: "On 17 December 1991, John Francis Nichols, 55, a well known wildlife dealer, was arrested with a friend by Customs Officials at Melbourne Airport, attempting to board a flight to New Zealand with 74 shingleback lizards and seven Bearded Dragons *(Pogona vitticeps)*. The lizards were packed into two suitcases, with their feet taped and hidden under a blanket when discovered by Customs officials."* At the time it was obvious that the lizards would be "laundered" and exported from New Zealand, since New Zealand had not as yet tightened up its wildlife regulations. Today, this would be illegal. In another case, according to Hoser's records, Peter and Rosaleen Robson of Freemantle, Australia, posted packages containing Western Bearded Dragons *(Pogona minima)* to reptile dealers in Denmark and Germany. They were intercepted before leaving Australia. These are just two documented cases of small numbers of beardies being smuggled.

* Reprinted with permission: Hoser, Raymond, Smuggled: The Underground Trade in Australia's Wildlife. Sydney, Australia: Kotaki Publishing, 1992.

not too long ago. Animals were easily transported by small, private boats from northern Australia to PNG. From PNG, they are then exported into the western part of this island, a state called Irian Jaya, which is part of Indonesia. From Irian Jaya, Indonesian animal exporters and freight consolidators shipped the animals to the Netherlands. Indonesia was a former Dutch colony, so there is a free flow of trade between the two nations. Once in the Netherlands, the animals were legally dispersed all over Europe (a common destination was Germany) and exported to other countries, such as the United States. While it is true that some Australian species are also naturally found in PNG, there are differences among the animals, and with a little bit of knowledge, they can be easily discerned. This is a moot point now, however, because PNG has also shut its borders to the export of reptiles and amphibians.

The Frilled Dragon, another native of Australia, joined Bearded Dragons in their status as stolen goods.

Another favorite fabrication is that an animal is a long-term captive or the descendant of captive-bred animals that were exported from Australia before they banned all exports. The ban went into effect more than thirty-five years ago, and few if any Australian herps that were legally exported before the ban were ever successfully captive-bred.

44

What happens to smuggled animals when they are confiscated? In some cases they are euthanized (the country of origin almost never wants them back), or they are given to schools, researchers, museums, zoos or licensed breeding or humane society facilities, which may adopt them out. When this occurs, takers are usually overwhelmed by large numbers of offspring—hence the great number of Bearded Dragons that are now available. Soon the offspring are either given away or sold and this is how such animals wind up in the hands of hobbyists . . . folks who would never think of getting involved with smuggling and are adamantly opposed to it. This is the best of all possible outcomes for confiscated animals. Smugglers should not be rewarded for their efforts, but the animals must not be made to pay for such illegal activity either! Hobbyists can enjoy and nurture the animals without having to engage in illegal conduct. Hobbyists are the proverbial "end-of-the-line" for such creatures, and without them the animals would surely be put to death.

Fads sometimes spur smuggling attempts. When a commercial appeared on Japanese television some years ago depicting Bearded Dragons as well as their cousins, the Australian Frilled Dragon, criminals are alleged to have succeeded in smuggling both species into that country. The TV ads spurred a "craze" and a demand for these animals as pets. It is important to resist the urge to have the "animal du jour." Buy the beer, not the "spokes-animal." This is not

---

HOPE FOR THE FUTURE

The Sydney Herald in Australia ran a story on July 6, 1998, announcing that a major Australian Senate inquiry into the commercial use of Australian wildlife is likely to recommend that export controls on native animals and plants be relaxed. The inquiry, however, is sure to spark a debate about the best way to control animal smuggling. It recommends that export bans be lifted for the first time since they became an Australian national policy back in the early 1960s. However, only birds and other animals that are captive-bred by licensed breeders are apt to fall within the proposed law. Some are also calling for a hefty export tax on such exports, proceeds of which would be used to promote wildlife conservation in Australia and to support a system of enforcement where captive breeding facilities are concerned. The added export tax is also likely to spur breeding attempts by overseas buyers who would gladly pay such fees to inject new genetic vigor into an aging and overworked gene pool among existing overseas stocks that are based on confiscated smuggled animals.

Most species of Bearded Dragon are neither rare nor endangered and they would make an excellent test export species for Australia, especially given their now worldwide popularity.

If confiscated by authorities, fortunate animals are given to organizations that will find them a good home.

only essential where illegal animals are concerned but also as to dangerous animals, such as venomous snakes or crocodilians!

Recent television commercials in the U.S. utilizing man-made look-alike frogs and Old World Chameleons have spurred an interest in both these animals. The Ninja Turtle cartoon craze spurred a heightened interest, especially among kids, for turtles. Fortunately, none of these animals are illegal to keep or particularly dangerous (save for the possibility of salmonella infection—particularly from turtles given to small children). Nonetheless, impulse buying of animals based on such public relations is still a bad idea. By definition, an impulse purchaser rarely stops to consider the animal's best interests.

chapter 6

Choosing
a Pet
Bearded Dragon

Bring Home a Healthy Beardie

Although adult beardies (6 to 12 inches in length) and adolescents (4 to 8 inches in length) are occasionally for sale, most of the time you will be offered baby dragons measuring about 3 to 4 inches including the tail. When selecting your pet, make sure that the animal is at least 4 to 6 weeks old (if possible) and eats both insect and vegetable matter with relish. Baby beardies should be fat, active when "spooked" or prodded and have a full tail. Both eyes should be wide open. There should be no obvious eye or mouth/jaw problems (see chapter 9) and no skin bumps other than the normal tubercles or bumpy processes found on these lizards. Because beardie babies are apt to nibble on each other, make sure your acquisition has all five toes, complete with tiny claws, on all four feet. Be especially wary of sellers (pet shops, swap-meet vendors or private breeders) that keep a bunch of baby dragons together in the same tank, as this practice tends to result in injured stock.

Some dragons will dominate others, prevent them from eating and will attack those that get in their way. In fact, it is an excellent idea to buy such a dominant lizard if you can identify it. Just make sure you keep it by itself.

Turn the baby dragon over and inspect its anal region. Make sure there are no feces or similar matter sticking to this area and that it is clean. If possible, ask the seller to feed the dragon in front of you. Also check for the presence of feces in the enclosure. It should be solid or semisolid and well-formed rather than excreted in a soft, amorphous mass, which is a sign of diarrhea.

Look for a fat baby beardie that runs off if you prod it.

Baby Beardies

Baby dragons sell for around $25 to $35 each. It is impossible to sex them as babies or juveniles, so if you are thinking of breeding them, you may have to buy four or five and raise them in individual enclosures. It is a bad idea, however, to breed dragons that have the same parent(s). It is best to buy from several different breeders so that when you are ready to breed them you will be assured of few or no genetic anomalies in the young, a situation more apt to occur if mating closely related animals.

Adult Dragons

Standard colored adult dragons cost from $100 to $300 each; young adult and adult dragons with different colors sell for more, but the price is apt to fall as they become more readily available. Prices change rapidly, and it is likely that by the time you read this they may be altogether different. If costs are of concern to you, the best thing to do is shop around.

Color Variations and Designer Beardies

Known as "morphs" or color variations, Bearded Dragons of the same species may exhibit different colors and patterns. Such differing colors and patterns often evolve as a result of natural selection over millennia. For example, a particular color variation might help beardies in a certain part of their territory to better disguise themselves against their background, thereby assisting them in escaping from predators. Beardies without this color variation are eaten, thus leaving mostly the color-adapted form to survive. Over many generations, the color-adapted beardies mate with each other until a new race of a different colored Bearded Dragon develops. An example occurs with Inland or Central Bearded Dragons *(Pogona vitticeps)* that occupy desert regions with a reddish-colored sand. Standard-colored beardies, usually a light grayish tan to off white don't blend in as well as reddish-colored dragons. The reddish-colored dragons survive, but the standard-colored animals are wiped out by predators. Breeders in the U.S. noticed that some of their dragons (probably the result of originally smuggled stock) exhibited these color variations, whereas others did not. Because beardies with such colors are in greater demand in the pet trade, breeders started breeding beardies to capitalize on such color variations.

> **DRAGONS ARE ON FIRE**
>
> According to Agama International, Bearded Dragons and other related agamid lizards are gaining rapidly in popularity and may surpass iguanas in the not too distant future as the most common "household" lizards. Agama International estimates that about 100,000 baby Bearded Dragons are produced and sold in North America annually. Breeders almost always sell out entire clutches within a few weeks of being hatched, so if you choose to obtain your dragons this way, you may have to put yourself on a waiting list!

49

According to experts who have bred many generations of these lizards, color variations such as these seem to be influenced by a variable set of genes rather than a simple set of dominant and/or recessive genes. Thus, no matter how hard they tried, breeders would always wind up with clutches that were at least 50 percent or more standard-colored and the balance the predicted color variation. Most of the color varieties developed to date include reddish, yellowish, golden and reddish-golden dragons. Breeders have also discovered a beardie with a red-gold head and pale blue-gray body and an unusual greenish-colored Inland Bearded Dragon. Selective breeding efforts have also resulted in baby dragons with reddish- or golden-colored heads and standard bodies.

Interestingly, some color variations, even if genetically based, are also dependent on dietary factors. An example of this occurred many years ago at the Bronx Zoo, which had a colony of pink flamingos that were losing their pink color and turning white. Zoo scientists soon discovered that these birds would retain their pink coloration if fed a diet rich in beta-carotene, a nutritional factor that was missing from their bird chow-based diet. In the wild, the birds found foods that helped provide this nutrient and would retain their pink coloration. Thus reddish-, yellowish-, orange- or golden-colored dragons may also depend on beta-carotene to maintain their coloration over time. Because beta-carotene and its close associate vitamin A can be toxic in high doses, they should be provided only once every two weeks in a scaled-down dose acceptable to a reptile of the beardie's size and type.

Red beardies evolved in areas of Australia where the sand is a reddish color. They are being bred in the U.S. for the pet trade, and you will occasionally find a red Bearded Dragon available.

Breeders who imported fresh stock from Germany some years ago also noticed that some of the Inland Bearded Dragons they received were unusually large and heavy bodied with lengths exceeding 2 feet. Dubbed "German Giants," these varieties were much bigger than standard beardies and had an iris that was silvery-gold. These gigantic Bearded Dragons also tend to produce unusually large clutches of up to sixty eggs at a time.

Snake breeders have for many years been experimenting with cross-breeding various natural color variations to obtain unusually patterned and colored snakes that do not, nor could, exist in the wild. These unusual reptiles are dubbed "designer snakes." Breeders are beginning to do the same with Bearded Dragons. One prominent, longtime breeder of beardies is developing the following "designer beardies:"

PICK A HEALTHY PET

When selecting your Bearded Dragon, look for an active lizard. Examine the eyes and make sure that they are wide open and clear. Check the beardie's body for any abnormal bumps. Look at the dragon's belly to be sure that the anal region is clean. Because baby beardies occasionally nibble on each other's feet, make sure that the one you bring home has all five toes, with claws, on all four feet.

- vivid orange eyelids with yellow facial highlights,
- orange beards with light buff brown bodies,
- juveniles with orange spots running down the back and
- barred side patterns leading to orange tiger patterned beardies.

Beardies with red heads are quite uncommon, but breeders are working to increase their numbers.

It won't be long before we'll have the same sort of beardie varieties that have been developed in snakes: Creamsicle beardies, zigzag beardies, black beardies, blue beardies, albino beardies and other variations we cannot even imagine. Whether this creative breeding will be good for the captive Bearded Dragon gene pool, a resource that is closed due to the illegality of obtaining fresh wild-caught stock, remains to be seen.

Some are breeding the unusually hardy German Giants mentioned above with some of the more colorful Bearded Dragons in the hope of creating color variations that are both beautiful as well as strong. The superior resistance to infectious disease of the German Giants is particularly noteworthy, and is believed to be the result of many years of captive breeding and the development of increasingly strong immune responses. If this work proved nothing else, it was that animals held in captivity are exposed to different sorts of infectious threats than those in the wild. This was demonstrated when these German Giants were bred with the progeny of recently captured wild-caught dragons. The early generations, at least, were not particularly more hardy or disease-resistant than one would expect. Based on these experiments, conferred immunities are apt to take many generations of captive breeding efforts to be fully realized and won't happen overnight.

Herp shows are held all over the country and are a great way to select the Bearded Dragon that you want.

Where to Get Your Bearded Dragon

A listing of some of the breeders and dealers of Bearded Dragons in the U.S. is provided in Chapter 12, "Resources." In order to buy from them, you may be asked to send a deposit on your purchase from a future clutch. These breeders are known to me and have an excellent reputation for breeding and selling top-quality animals. For your own protection, be sure to ascertain their policies and terms before you buy, so as to prevent any misunderstandings. If you want to see the animal before you buy it, then your next best option is to attend a large local or national swap meet or wait until your local pet shop obtains some Bearded Dragons. Your local herpetological society may also be a source of information on someone in your area who is breeding and selling Bearded Dragons.

Beardies on the Net

You can contact breeders and other keepers of Bearded Dragons on the Internet. There is even a listserv forum devoted solely to beardies: pogona@lists. best.com. Chapter 12, "Resources," provides complete instructions on how to join. Here you can contact breeders of Bearded Dragons as well as obtain references on their reliability from third-party members via private mail. In the public forum, you can also discuss Bearded Dragon issues, ask care and keeping questions and perhaps even find takers for the results of your own breeding projects. Why not share your own experiences—both good and bad—with fellow Bearded Dragon enthusiasts? This is a fun and educational way to learn more about Bearded Dragons as well as to offer advice based on your own efforts.

Caring

for Your

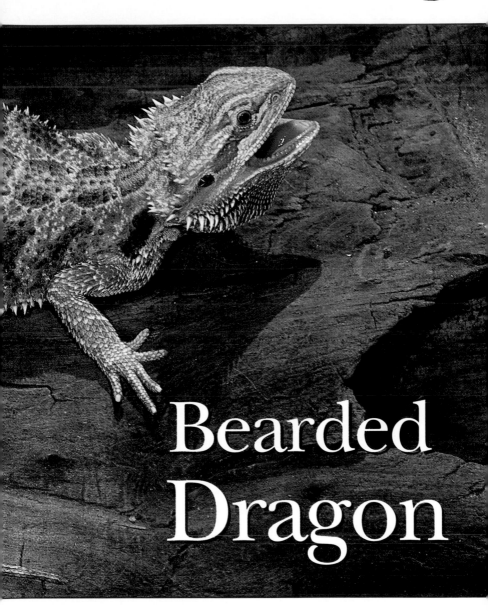

Bearded Dragon

Housing
Bearded Dragons

All Bearded Dragon enthusiasts agree that these lizards appreciate very sizable housing.

Size Does Matter

Baby dragons should be kept in enclosures at least 3 to 4 feet in length and at least 12 inches wide (a bigger cage is fine). Adults need larger quarters. A cage that is a minimum of 6 feet in length, 16 to 20 inches wide and at least 18 inches high is recommended for one or two adult dragons. Adults of the smaller species can be kept in caging similar to that recommended for baby and sub-adult or juvenile dragons. Beardies like to stretch their legs, so don't hesitate to provide them with the most commodious enclosure that your space allows.

Custom-made cages can be built according to commercially or personally drawn up plans. Measure the area where you plan to keep the enclosure, so that you can be sure that the cage has the right dimensions.

I keep my dragons by a window with blinds. The blinds shut out the light and heat if it becomes excessive, but permit unfiltered sunlight to rain down on the dragons during the warmer months of the year.

Indoor Caging

Indoor caging can be most expediently created from an all-glass aquarium fitted with a screen cover. An off-the-shelf reptile cage or a custom-built cage are also possibilities. As a species that inhabits arid or dry habitats, beardies don't need waterproof cages. Fish tanks discarded because of leaks, wooden, plastic or melamine cages and custom-made enclosures made of wood, glass and screening (for ventilation) can all be adapted for Bearded Dragon housing. Whatever your choice, just make sure it is large enough to house whatever number of dragons you intend to keep in it, and that it provides for easy maintenance.

CAGE COVERS

A mesh screen is the cover of choice for your beardies—screening allows for plenty of needed ventilation and permits unfiltered sunlight or artificial ultraviolet (UV) A and B light to shine through. Under no circumstances should a glass cover, which blocks UV rays, be used. Moreover, glass covers cause the air to stagnate and cause the buildup of humidity and noxious gases that could be harmful to your dragons. Because they retain excessive heat and humidity, all-glass covers also promote fungal growth.

Clearly, covers should always be made of screening, or "hardware cloth" as it is occasionally called. Covers can be purchased in pet shops for most aquarium tank sizes. If your cage is an odd size, it may be necessary to build your own frame and cover it with screening yourself. Besides keeping dragons and feeder insects such as crickets in, such covers keep out inquisitive children and other household pets. They are also useful for placement of basking and full-spectrum lighting (see below). Outdoors, they are a must to protect your lizards from cats, possums, raccoons, predatory birds and the like.

If your tank is high enough, with at least 6 to 8 inches between the highest perch (if you provide perches) and the top, you might also consider using no lid at all. While dragons are superb climbers of wooden and rocky surfaces, they do not jump nor can they obtain purchase on the smooth glass, plastic or wooden sides of an enclosure, so there is little risk of escape. However, other household pets can get into the cage, including cats and perhaps your dog . . . and either may not be above trying to eat your beardie or, at the very least, checking it out by biting into it. If you have no other pets, you should consider an open top. If a perch or rocky outcrop is used, it can be placed in the center of the cage, well away from the walls. In this location, it cannot serve as a "ladder" for your dragon to climb over the top.

A screen cover is a good choice— it lets in light, allows for the air to circulate and keeps a dragon safe from other household pets.

CAGE HEIGHT—HOW HIGH IS HIGH?

Height is important because beardies love to climb and perch on posts and branches. In a captive situation, the enclosure should be at least 2 to 2½ feet high. Remember that beardies love to do three things: sprint, climb and perch above ground level. Although they will stay in one place for seemingly hours on end, basking or soaking up the heat from above or from the substrate, there will be times when the lizards would like to take off for a little run or climb among some branches heavy enough to support them.

COMMUNITY CAGING?

Bearded Dragons are territorial. If you are keeping more than one lizard per enclosure, you must give them plenty of room to call their own, including separate feeding stations. You may, nonetheless, find that you have to separate them as you notice the submissive members becoming weaker or damaged by attacks made by the dominant member(s) of the group. Because your lid is apt to be screening, make sure that your beardie cannot reach the screen and rub its snout raw trying to nose its way out.

SUBSTRATES

Bottom cover for indoor cages can be as simple as white, unprinted paper toweling or unprinted newspaper, a layer of #30 silica sand or smooth, water-worn aquarium gravel, sand or pebbles. Many substrates are dangerous to beardies because they accidentally may swallow some of it when feeding—as some substrates

Make sure that the substrate that you use is digestible, as it is likely that your Bearded Dragon will swallow some of it while eating.

are indigestible, this can result in intestinal blockage or fecal impaction. One commercial substrate, Bone-Aid Calci-Sand, is completely digest-ible, provides much needed calcium and reduces the risk of intestinal blockage. (See T-Rex Products in chapter 12.) Astroturf and similar carpet materials have also been advocated as a substrate. Such weaves must

be tight to prevent beardies from catching their nails in the cloth and ripping them off in an attempt to break free.

PLANTS

Silk plants are recommended, as your dragons are apt to eat live plants. Although the latter may be more aesthetically pleasing, some may be poisonous to your animals. Some plants naturally contain toxins; others have been treated or sprayed by growers. If you do choose to include live plants, be sure to thoroughly wash them before potting them in your vivarium.

Artificial plants pose little risk to your beardies and can be quite attractive. They do, however, have to be removed and washed from time to time. For ease of handling, all plants should be anchored in their own pots or soil so that they can be easily removed when necessary. Otherwise, you may have to uproot or upset a large amount of your dragon's terrain for such an operation.

Be sure that your enclosure provides a shelter box to sleep in.

CAGE FURNISHINGS

Beardies love to climb and perch. They like to survey all that they can see from above. Scientists classify them as "semiarboreal" because they do not ascend high into trees as truly arboreal animals do but prefer perches that are just a few feet off the ground. In a cage, a well-anchored, heavy-duty driftwood branch needs to be only 4 to 6 inches above the substrate for your beardie's climbing enjoyment. You can also construct naturalistic rock formations for your beardie. Beardies will even settle for sitting atop their shelter boxes or leaning against them, backs to the light, for the purpose of soaking up rays. A variety of naturalistic artificial rock formations, caves and shelters are sold in pet shops, many of which will serve your beardie well.

Basking constructions should be kept 2 or more feet away from any direct heating lamps, so that dragons can bask at a distance without overheating. It is useful to check the temperature on the basking spot, being certain that even after an hour or more of light, the area doesn't exceed 85° to 90°F.

BEARDIES LIKE BEDS, LIZARD STYLE

Shelter boxes (beds to Bearded Dragons), are available in both naturalistic rocky designs or as no-frills plastic containers with doorways, that, when turned upside-down, form a shelter for your dragon to sleep in. While these no-frills containers are not pretty, Bearded Dragons don't seem to care. They serve their purpose well. More elaborate shelters benefit the human viewer more than the dragons. They can make do with just about any old shelter, so long as it is big enough to accommodate them.

LIGHTING THE LIZARD OF OZ

Exposing your dragons to eight to ten hours of natural daylight a day is probably the best way to ensure they receive adequate amounts of light. Natural daylight provides UV-B and UV-A rays, which help in the synthesis of vitamin D_3. This, in turn, aids in the appropriate metabolism of calcium, necessary for healthy bone formation and growth. Absence of vitamin D_3 causes a variety of bone-related conditions, which are discussed in more detail in chapter 9.

Some experts feel that by feeding beardies a diet rich in both animal and plant nutrients, you can eliminate the need for either sunlight or a full-spectrum fluorescent substitute. I have found that adult dragons fare well under incandescent light only and do not rely on or need either sunlight or full-spectrum lighting if fed a properly supplemented diet. On the other hand, baby beardies kept under this regimen did not grow as fast or as robustly as those receiving either sunlight or artificial full-spectrum lighting in spite of a similar diet and the same supplementation (Triple-Calcium and vitamin D_3).

As noted previously, the UV-B light emitted by the sun or such special full-spectrum bulbs that produce UV-B is involved in vitamin D_3 synthesis in the skin that leads to improved bone growth and formation. UV-A light is

believed to produce a positive environmental stimulus, causing captive beardies to eat better, maintain activity levels and perhaps even to breed. UV-A rays are detected by the third eye (or pineal eye), and probably play a role in the lizard's circadian rhythms, as well as stimulating hormone production and release.

If natural sunlight is not available, artificial full-spectrum lightbulbs (available at pet shops) should be placed in a shielded fixture and set atop the screen cover of the enclosure. The light should be left on for fourteen hours a day during the spring

Full-spectrum lightbulbs may be placed on the screen cover of your Bearded Dragon's enclosure if natural sunlight is not available.

and summer and for ten hours daily during the fall and winter. Such lighting is a critical factor in raising baby dragons to adulthood and is undoubtedly essential in promoting mating and breeding cycles in adults. It is important to remember that these bulbs may go on shining long after they lose their ability to produce UV-B and UV-A. It is important, therefore, to replace them every six months or so, regardless of whether or not they are burned out. If you use many of such bulbs, it may pay to invest in a meter that indicates whether the light is producing the desired or requisite levels of UV radiation.

If natural sunlight is used, be sure that it shines indirectly into your dragon's enclosure through screening or an open top. Regular glass filters out essential UV rays and, in addition, can result in overheating of the entire enclosure. (In short, a glass top and direct sunlight can cook your lizards!) If your enclosure is indoors and you wish to keep the window closed in the winter but still derive the benefit of sunlight for your dragons, you can purchase a windowpane of special glass that allows the passage of ultraviolet rays. Such glass is expensive but you may not need to purchase a large quantity to achieve your purpose. Moreover, in the long run, you may save money by obviating the need to buy special fluorescent tubes. Contact your window dealer or contractor for more information.

PROVIDING HEAT

As mentioned previously, Bearded Dragons in the wild thermoregulate, thereby sustaining a comfortable temperature. There is little difference between what happens in the wild and what your dragon does in captivity save for one big thing—in captivity, you are in charge of providing the heat. You control your beardie's thermal environment, whether cool or hot, so it is important that you provide the absolute best conditions possible. These conditions allow your pet to continue doing what it normally would do were it scampering around the Australian outback.

Outdoors, Bearded Dragons bask in the sunlight to warm up. At home, you must provide both warm and cool spots for your beardie.

In order to fully understand how heat or cold is provided to captive reptiles, it is helpful to conceptualize the means by which thermal changes or gradients can be provided.

Heat can come from above by means of:

- incandescent lights,
- infrared bulbs (e.g. heat lamps),
- nonlight-emitting screw-in ceramic heaters,
- natural sunlight.

Heat can come from below by means of:

- electrically powered heating pads,
- heat tape, available in various widths,
- so-called "pig blankets," which are large rubberized or fiberglass-coated heavy-duty heating pads; especially useful for outdoor enclosures,
- hot rocks,
- environmental heat, such as baseboard heaters, room heaters, radiators—standard household heating systems (gas, steam, electric).

All electrically powered heating products that produce heat from below can be thermostatically controlled. Such devices can be made to turn off or turn on depending on the temperature registered electronically at the surface of the enclosure. Hot rocks, which are ceramic, "naturalistic" looking stone formations with built-in heating elements, have a reputation of developing hot spots, overheating and burning your reptile. If they are functioning properly and if they do not overheat, hot rocks can be an asset to any lizard that obtains its belly warmth from below. But be very careful if you give your pet access to hot rocks— your lizard may not consciously be aware that there is too much heat coming from below until that heat permeates its body and reaches higher thermoregulatory centers in the brain. It is this quirk of reptile physiology that has caused

**HUMIDITY?
DON'T SWEAT IT**

It is not necessary to acquire humidity measuring equipment, and you should do nothing to promote humidity buildup. Only *Pogona barbata* is known to live in habitats with higher than usual relative humidity, but this species and all the rest do best in an arid habitat. Good ventilation of the cage coupled with minimal water inside will accomplish the aridity you are seeking for your dragon.

them to endure burns on their belly scales before they realize the heating device beneath them is too hot. Because you will not be able to watch your beardie all the time, you are probably better off relying on alternative heating methods.

If you want to provide vertical temperature zones, place a reflector and incandescent bulb at either end of the enclosure and focus the bulb across the cage at mid-level. Your Bearded Dragon can climb up to the heat if it likes.

All reptile and amphibian enclosures, including those for Bearded Dragons, must have areas that are hot, areas that are cooler and areas that are cooler still. These are known as temperature gradients and Bearded Dragons must be allowed a choice of locations to rest and remain, each with a different temperature. The zones of varying temperatures can exist either in the horizontal or vertical plane, although it is much more difficult to arrange them vertically than horizontally. Nature, however, does this quite nicely. You can achieve a vertical temperature zone in captivity by placing a reflector at one end and an incandescent bulb at the other end of the enclosure and focusing it at mid-level straight across the cage. Ground-dwelling reptiles, such as snakes and many terrestrial lizards, do not benefit from layers of heat at different heights but beardies, as semiarboreal species, are apt to appreciate having a range of vertical heat levels.

If you opt to use a nonlight-emitting heat source from above, such as an infrared bulb, which emits only red light, or any number of ceramic nonlight-emitting heating coils, you must use specially insulated, heavy-duty reflectors and sockets to absorb the excessive heat produced and to help to prevent fires. No flammable portion of your enclosure should come in direct or even close contact with any of these devices. This includes the plastic frames of all-glass aquariums, the plastic frames of screen covers, the screen covers themselves (especially if made of plastic netting), anything made of wood or anything else that can either melt or burn. In addition, all cage fixtures should be secure and incapable of toppling over. One unfortunate Iguana owner came home to find his house on fire only to learn that the fire was started by his lizard! The Iguana had knocked over the heat lamp, which was in close proximity to some window curtains. Always "think" in terms of fire prevention when setting up such arrangements.

If you are the forgetful type or won't be home when the heat from above is no longer needed (usually after nightfall), it may be useful to have fixtures plugged into timers that will turn them off in your absence. Bearded Dragons expect temperature drops after nightfall; this is when they become inactive and rest.

> **PEOPLE THERMOREGULATE, TOO**
>
> By turning on air conditioners, radiators, electric heaters, standing close to the fire or away from it, taking a cold shower, going into and out of the water (pool, lake or sea) or escaping the heat with an umbrella or awning, people thermoregulate, too. There is little difference between these human behaviors and the way reptiles thermoregulate. When establishing your lizard's thermal environment, try to remember how you feel when waiting for the bus on a winter day or when you have a power failure in August. Your beardie will appreciate your sensitivity.

Optimal Beardie Temperatures

Daytime environmental temperatures should range from 80° to 85°F. Basking spots should be hotter, ranging from 90° to a maximum of 93°F. At night, the heat source for the basking spots should be turned off. Environmental temperature should be allowed to drop to anywhere from 75° to 65°F.

Supplemental Heating

If you keep your house cooler at night, especially during the wintertime in North America, it may be necessary to provide supplemental heating for your Bearded

Dragons. You can do this through the use of red or dark blue incandescent bulbs, infrared bulbs, non-light-emitting ceramic heating elements and under-cage heating pads or heat tape. If you know your household temperature is apt to drop below 70°F during the night, you can arrange to have these devices turn on either by timer or via thermostat. Thermostats will shut off the heat element if overheating occurs while you (and your dragon) are asleep, so this is the preferred alternative. Set the thermostat to cut off the heating elements when temperatures reach 65° or 70°F. It will turn them back on if temperatures drop below 65°F.

Monitoring Heat

A good mercury, chemical or electronic thermometer is a must to accurately monitor the temperature in your Bearded Dragon enclosure. Trying to estimate the temperature inside an enclosure is impossible because our body temperature prevents us from evaluating how the temperature feels to the dragon. The best thermometers to invest in are battery-operated, electronic devices with probes that can be inserted into the tank while the screen read-out remains outside. Check the resource section for dealers of this equipment.

Cage Cleaning and Maintenance

Bearded Dragons will eat copious amounts of food on a daily basis, and they will foul their substrate and water dish (if one is provided) just as rapidly. Therefore, all fecal material and uneaten or leftover vegetable matter should be removed every day. In addition, fouled water bowls should be removed, drained and rinsed on an as-needed basis. At some point, substrate material will become totally inundated with dried-up bits of uneaten food and small amounts of fecal material/urine that you can't clean up. This requires you to replace it in its entirety. Cage furniture, such as shelters, driftwood perches or rock formations, should also be removed periodically and cleaned. The glass walls of any beardie cage should be wiped down inside and out with a water-dampened paper towel whenever necessary.

Other maintenance chores include watering live plants, trimming off dead leaves and, if your beardeds nibble on them, replacement of the entire plant! You should also monitor your heating system and check temperatures throughout the enclosure a part of your daily or every-other-day chores.

Free Roaming

Some hobbyists devote a room in their home in which their pet can free roam. If you opt for this type of "housing," be very certain that the room is tightly sealed so that your lizard doesn't escape.

A number of lizard owners such as those with Iguanas and Monitor Lizards advocate allowing them, if large enough, to free roam in the house. This is a reasonable idea but only one secure room should be devoted to this purpose, whether for adult dragons, Iguanas or Monitors. Needless to say, there should be no holes or escape routes large enough to accommodate passage of your lizard. And while there is no proof beardies shed salmonella, as do other lizards, bear in mind they may do so. Therefore, other pets, such as dogs and cats, as well as small children, toddlers and babies, should be prohibited from entering such a habitat or playing in it. A lock on the door is a very wise idea if children "free roam" elsewhere in the house.

Outdoor Vivariums and Greenhouses

In some drier parts of the U.S., it may be possible to house your dragons in outdoor enclosures or pens during the warmer months. Such enclosures should provide shelter, be protected from predators such as birds, raccoons, foxes, dogs and the like and should be heated at night if temperatures drop below 65°F. A screen cover is the best type of security measure as long as it is fitted

tightly. It allows your dragons to bask in unfiltered sunlight during the day and nothing can be healthier for
them.

Many breeders feel such an arrangement helps stimu-
late breeding cycles, and young beardies will benefit by
enhanced growth in larger outdoor vivariums as well.
Outdoor vivariums in areas of heavy rainfall and high
humidity might be suitable if you provide the dragons
with a high, dry place to shel-
ter in the event of rain.
Indoor greenhouses may
have too much humidity
unless well ventilated, usually
by rooftop windows that can
be slung open.

HEAT FOR OUTDOOR ENCLOSURES

Heating dragon enclosures
outdoors in colder climates is
highly problematic. If your
heating system fails in the
middle of the night when
temperatures are plunging
into the 20s, 30s or even 40s,
you can wake up to find your
dragon dead. It is not recom-
mended that you keep dragons outdoors year-round in
any climate where day or nighttime temperatures fall
below 60° to 65°F. In some parts of the U.S., such as
southern California and Florida, dragons can be kept
in well-protected outdoor compounds virtually year-
round, but should be brought indoors on those few
days where temperatures may drop below the 60s.
During the day, outdoor enclosures and greenhouses
are heated by natural sunlight (if there is sun—if not,
artificial, thermostatically controlled heating must be
available). Sunlight can over-heat a greenhouse during
warmer months (in North America: March through
October), so such structures must have roof windows

*If you live in an
arid climate, you
may consider hous-
ing your lizard in
an outdoor vivar-
ium with a secure
screen cover.*

that can be opened or other panels that are screened off but which will permit adequate ventilation or cooling airflow.

If you live in a climate where keeping lizards outside is not appropriate, you may nonetheless succeed in doing so if you have a heated greenhouse with an alarm that is triggered if the heating system should fail. You must be certain that the enclosure will retain heat, even on cold days. Year-round enclosures should be closed on four sides, have a natural or sandy substrate under which heating pads can be placed and have a screen cover. Caves or upside-down wooden or plastic boxes with entrances cut into them can serve as shelter from the elements. During the winter, the substrate can be enhanced by placing a 1-foot-deep loosely-packed layer of alfalfa, which will give dragons the opportunity of digging into the substrate for insulation. If there are heavy rains or snowfall, you must move your dragons indoors for the duration of such harsh weather conditions.

LEAVING BEARDIES HOME ALONE

Although it is not a good idea to leave any animal home alone for any length of time, short trips away can be safely taken so long as your beardies are fed and checked on at least every two or three days by a substitute caretaker or yourself. Unlike some species of fish or amphibians that must be fed daily or even more frequently, beardies can go for several days without food or fresh water (although they'd rather not). Bearded Dragons have developed such resilience in order to cope with the harsh circumstances of their natural desert or rocky scrubland existence in the wild. Nonetheless, they will eat and drink every day, even several times a day, if given the opportunity. If there is no compelling reason to skip a few days, don't.

SUBSTRATES

Natural grassy or soil substrates should be cleaned regularly. Keep an eye on the substrate to be certain that it remains fresh. All uneaten food and fecal material should be scooped up and used in mulch, as fertilizer for flower beds, or otherwise properly discarded. You should routinely rake and turn the soil to a depth of at least 8 inches. By keeping the soil loose, the dragons will be able to dig in if they so choose. It is important that the dragons be able to protect and insulate themselves by digging into the substrate—if it becomes hardened and packed down, they may die in the night from cold temperatures. A heated shelter or underground heating pad will also help prevent such disasters. Temperatures and heating systems including thermostats should be checked at least once a day, preferably just before nightfall.

If you really want to provide a comfortable (and attractive) habitat for your Bearded Dragons, you may consider building them a specially designed outdoor vivarium or greenhouse. The enclosure can be planted, landscaped and have free-flowing water or misting/grass sprinklers (to be used once or twice a day to water plants and provide "rainfall" for dragons to drink). It can be heated by fan-operated gas heaters, electrical heating pads or even hot water pipes. The frame can be made of treated wood or aluminum, to which a sturdy hardware cloth (preferably rubberized) should be added. The mesh should be small enough to prevent dragons from obtaining a toe-hold and climbing on it, as they might be apt to tear it (creating an escape route) or tear off toenails while moving about.

Hobbyists with a good-size yard may build a con tained vivarium for their Bearded Dragons. Mesh siding permits air to circulate throughout the enclosure, and should be tightly woven to prevent the beardies from climbing up the walls.

All outdoor vivariums should be deeply set into the ground, at least to a depth of 18 inches or more, to prevent dragons from tunneling their way out. As a precautionary measure, you may want to place a treated wooden platform as the outdoor vivarium or greenhouse floor, and cover it with 1 or 2 feet of soil. If the beardies dig in that deep, they will be stopped by the hidden flooring below.

chapter 8

Feeding
Bearded
Dragons

Ideally, Bearded Dragons should be fed and given water on a daily basis. Some hobbyists feed their beardies two or even three meals a day. Three meals a day is a healthy feeding schedule for these lizards, if two of those meals consist of greens. It is helpful when discussing beardie feeding and nutrition to understand some special terms that apply to their dietary preferences:

omnivorous—eating both animal and vegetable matter

herbivorous—eating only vegetable matter

carnivorous—eating only animal matter

foliovorous—leaf eating

frugivorous—fruit eating

insectivorous—insect eating

Beardies are all of the above and more. Their willing
ness to consume all types of food is one of the attrib-
utes that makes them so easy to care for. They are
dietary generalists rather than specialists and can be
coached to eat specially prepared food out of a jar.
They will even eat other lizards, including babies of
their own species, so they can also be considered can-
nibalistic. Adult dragons will eat baby (and very young)
mice. Like humans, beardies will eat just about anything they find palatable. But this doesn't mean a
steady diet of one food or another is necessarily good
for them. Just like people, Bearded Dragons do best on
a varied diet. Fatty, animal-based foods should be fed
in moderation. Fortunately, beardies like their veggies,
and vegetables should form the basis of their diet with
animal-based foods offered two or three times a week
to meet their need for animal-based protein and other
nutritional factors. A balanced, well-crafted diet will
help your Bearded Dragon to live long and prosper.

Veggies

Vegetables should be chopped into a suitable size,
depending on the size of the animal being fed. Baby
dragons need finely chopped veggies, juveniles more
coarsely chopped food and adults can swallow most
vegetables in human-sized portions with little difficulty.
Among the vegetables recommended for dragons are:

- carrots (raw and shredded, about 1 to 2 ounces a
  week)

- collard greens

- dandelion greens (leaves and flowers)

- frozen mixed veggies (carrots, beans and peas,
  thawed)

- hibiscus blooms and other nontoxic flowers (as an occasional treat)

- kale

- mustard greens

A small amount of finely chopped tender baby spinach leaves can be added to the diet of developing dragons to provide additional iron. Spinach, broccoli and other cruciferous vegetables should be fed in very small amounts no more than once a week. Too much of these foods can be harmful to your beardies. You can round out the diet by adding chopped, thawed mixed vegetables.

Various lettuces (iceberg, romaine, bib, Boston and red or green leaf) should not be fed except in an emergency. Dragons love such lettuces but they hold little nutritional value for them unless amply supplemented with sprinkled calcium or other vitamin/mineral supplements devised for reptiles.

Feed vegetables chopped to an appropriate size for your pet. This baby beardie's leafy greens are finely chopped.

Commercial Lizard Foods

A number of manufacturers have developed pelleted foods that can be fed to beardies out of the jar. (See Chapter 12, "Resources," for more information on these products.) These prepared foods can be blended with regular vegetable diets. To date, I have not been able to get any Bearded Dragon to eat a commercial food without combining it with something else. If you coach your Bearded Dragon to eat these foods without resorting to this kind of trickery, it is still important that you don't rely on them to the exclusion of other dietary items. At this time, there are no long-term published studies indicating that commercial foods are adequate or superior as a sole source of nutrition for Bearded Dragons. Some beardie keepers report that their dragons gobble up pellets, others find that they refuse them and some even spit them out if they eat them by accident!

A variety of nutritious vegetables should be the basis of a dragon's diet.

Insects

Bearded Dragons will eat a wide variety of insects. If you catch the insects yourself, you must be absolutely certain they haven't been exposed to any insecticides, herbicides or chemical fertilizers. Most insects suitable for feeding to lizards can be purchased as commercially bred and cultured. A list of such suppliers is included in chapter 12. Pet shops, particularly those that sell reptiles, can also be relied upon to stock suitable feeder insects.

You should feed feeder insects a highly nutritional dietary supplement before feeding them to your

Caring for Your
Bearded Dragon

beardies. This is a simple process known as "gut load-ing." The insect becomes a vehicle or carrier of the nutrients that it has consumed. Crickets, mealworms, and small mice can be fed a diet of high-quality rodent

chow. Crickets, a favorite of Bearded Dragons, can also be fed one of the com-mercially prepared high calcium/vitamin D_3 cricket diets. The above-mentioned pellets designed for lizards also make a good gut-loader food for crickets. Place a handful of the pel-lets in a jar cap, spray them lightly with water and soon your feeder crickets will be all over them. Vitamin C is provided by giving your crickets some sliced oranges; this also provides them with fluids and eliminates the need for a messy water-ing sponge. Avoid water dishes in your crickets' housing, as the crickets fall in, swim around and then quickly drown.

Some beardies en-joy commercial pellets, while others reject them. If your pet likes pellets, be sure to include other healthful food in the diet.

Crickets are a popular feeder insect for Bearded Dragons. These two young beardies delicately share a cricket meal.

Gut-loaded insects should be fed to your dragons as quickly as possible after they've been fed their enriched diet. By delaying, insects will pass the nutrients before your dragon has a chance to gobble them up.

Feeding Babies—From Newborn to 4 Months of Age

You have to be careful about overfeeding baby dragons. Although their growth is rapid during this time and they need plenty of food, like babies of all species they need to have smaller meals, and to be fed more frequently, than their adult counterparts.

Baby dragons have hearty appetites. A baby dragon would not hesitate, for example, to attempt to overpower and eat an adult cricket. The result, however, could be disastrous for your lizard. Its small diges-

A tiny young cricket is just right for a baby beardie.

tive system is apt to become injured by the tougher parts of the cricket (such as their serrated legs). Moreover, should it manage to stuff such a morsel into its mouth, the bulk of the food in the beardie's stomach can put pressure on the nerves in the lower part of the lizard's body, causing temporary, or worse, a permanent rear leg paralysis. Therefore, you need to feed baby beardies crickets that are only a few weeks old or no larger than ½ inch in body length. Cricket suppliers grade their crickets using a numbering system and sell all sizes.

If feeding mealworm larvae to baby beardies, select smaller, just-molted specimens. Just-molted mealworms are creamy white in color, whereas larvae with tougher, chitinous shells are yellow or brownish-yellow in color. This tough exterior is difficult for baby dragons to digest and can easily cause a gastrointestinal blockage that could be fatal.

Another good, tender choice for baby dragons is the larvae of the waxmoth. These are relatively small, and they are so soft that they are not a problem to digest. It is also important to gut load insects and dust them two or three times a week with specially formulated reptile vitamin/mineral supplement powders. Some of these are fine enough to stick on the insect for several minutes while they are being offered to your dragon.

Conventional wisdom indicates that during this developmental stage, dragons need a significant amount of animal protein (in contrast with the nutrients in vegetable matter). Be that as it may, don't hesitate to offer them vegetables and get them started early on a healthy diet. Vegetable matter should be finely chopped with a food chopper or sharp knife and offered in small quantities in a tiny dish (a large bottle cap works nicely). Direct the dragon's nose to the dish and then leave it alone and allow it to discover a taste for veggies. A veggie meal should be offered every other day at this stage.

> **FEED BABY DRAGONS FREQUENTLY**
>
> It was noted in the prior chapter that dragons make good pets—if you need to go away for a day or two they can be left food and water and be in good shape when you return. After three days, adults should be fed again. However, this is not the case with baby beardies; babies need to be fed twice daily (at a minimum) during their first six months of life. You cannot escape the daily chore of feeding baby dragons without impairing their development or worse yet, seeing them die. Therefore, if you must be away from home either bring them with you (in a small plastic carrier/terrarium) or be sure a trusted friend or relative will take up your feeding chores when you are absent.

At least one breeder reports that he has had unusually good luck feeding newborn beardies termites, although they are difficult to find (he raises his own by burying a rotten piece of wood out back). He makes sure each baby dragon gets a few termites daily and claims that he has never lost a hatchling due to failure to thrive.

Feeding Adults—From 4 Months to Adulthood

Once your dragons are around 4 months old, veggies should be offered every other feeding. At 8 months to full adulthood, they should be eating greens at least once every day and animal protein around two or three times a week. It is helpful if you douse the vegetable matter with a little extra water. This is a good way to get fluids into your dragons and will be appreciated. You can scale back supplementing insects or veggies with vitamin/mineral powders to once a week when full adulthood is reached. Note, however, that breeding females need extra nutrients for embryo, yolk and eggshell formation (see chapter 10).

Adult dragons can be fed crickets that are 6 weeks old or older, larger mealworms, king mealworms *(Zoophobas morio)* or "zoophobias" as they are commonly known. Waxmoth larvae (waxworms) and other bugs may also be fed; but avoid hard-shelled beetles, as they can cause intestinal blockage. Similarly, deeply colored, yellowish-brown mealworms have a tough, chitinous outer skin that is indigestible and that could also cause intestinal problems for your pet. Whenever possible, feed light-colored, or freshly molted, mealworms that have not yet developed a tough outer layer. Pinky (newborn) mice and fuzzy mice can also be eaten by young adults, and larger adult dragons will even subdue and eat young mice. These animal foods should be fed only once every two or three days. Feed coarsely chopped or unchopped greens and mixed veggies daily.

Some Bearded Dragons are placid enough to be fed by hand. This beardie enjoys a giant mealworm.

It is important to feed a variety of food and to offer as many foods as possible—do not become dependent on just one type of food. Vegetables should be the main component of your dragon's diet. Although dragons will relish young mice, they are high in fat content and your dragons run the risk of becoming obese as a result of a steady diet of such foods.

As dietary generalists, Bearded Dragons have been known to eat small birds, eggs and fish on a regular basis. A willingness to eat fish is surprising, as most Bearded Dragons live in areas of little or no water, let alone in the presence of large stocks of small fish they are capable of catching. In captivity, this is a different matter. Feeder fish or even pieces of fish destined for people can be placed in a shallow dish of water and the beardies will readily gobble them up. Fish is high in nutrients and is a good occasional change of diet for beardies, but tropical fish may pose a danger. Tropical fish often harbor a parasite called *Microspora* that Bearded Dragons can contract. There is no treatment to rid fish or beardies of this parasite and the disease can be fatal. (See chapter 9 for more information on parasites.)

SUPPLEMENTS

There is a bewildering array of vitamin/mineral supplements on the market for reptiles, so it's often necessary to put on those reading glasses and take a long, hard look at ingredient lists. Avoid products or firms that don't provide this information. For calcium and vitamin D_3 supplementation, I use a triple calcium product (with no vitamin A or other vitamins/minerals).

One way to supplement your dragon's diet is to feed crickets dusted with vitamins.

Although there are some excellent supplements available, your dragons should get nearly all the vitamins and proteins they need from a varied diet of animal and vegetable matter. For baby and juvenile dragons, supplements should be given on one feeding every day. When your dragons reach a length of 8 to 10 inches, their growth will slow down, and you can begin supplementing their diet every other day. Once adulthood is reached, the lizards are at their full size, and supplements can be added weekly. Breeding females should receive supplements every day or every other day until two weeks after egg-laying. If you expect to breed a particular female several times in one season, you should supplement her diet daily.

Watering Your Beardies

Water is essential to life everywhere. Reptiles and amphibians that live under conditions of little or no rainfall and in the absence of surface ground water adapt by conserving what water they can from their food and excreting their urine in either a solid state or semisolid state along with their feces. Often you will see white pieces of a dry, "powdery" substance in your dragon's enclosure. This is waterless urine. It is composed of uric acid and other waste products that normally would be excreted dissolved in fluid.

The traditional means of offering water is to provide your lizards with a water dish. Such a dish can be bought in a pet shop in decorative styles or you can use a shallow glass ashtray or even an upside-down jar or bottle cap. Not all dragons drink from water dishes, so you must make sure that they are using it for this purpose. Some beardies will use their water dishes as a toilet (the dish must be cleaned right away when this occurs). Often, dragons will throw substrate into their dish as they wander through it. Clearly, water dishes tend to get fouled quickly and they must be kept scrupulously clean— if not, they will soon turn into a dangerous source of bacterial and fungal contamination. If you cannot coach your dragon to drink from a water dish,

Dragons obtain fluids from the insects that they eat, but animal foods are not a sufficient source of liquids. Be sure that your Bearded Dragon has access to fresh, clean water at all times.

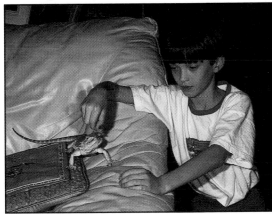

it is best to dispense with it and rely on watering down veggies or spraying as a means of getting water into your lizard. Dragons may have low levels of bacteria in their feces that will concentrate and bloom in water dishes. By drinking water contaminated in this way, the lizards will obtain higher doses of enteric bacteria that could result in diarrhea, other gastrointestinal problems or even in their death. Such germs may also be transmitted to people. It is very important, therefore, to make sure that water dishes are kept absolutely spotless at all times. Handle dirty dishes with care, washing, disinfecting and rinsing them well in very hot water in a sink not used for food preparation or human dish and utensil washing.

If your local tap water does not taste good, or if you would not drink it yourself, be sure to give bottled spring or noncarbonated mineral water to your dragons. The trace elements in such waters will be beneficial to your pets and you will not risk harming them with local tap or well water. Distilled or purified waters are devoid of such elements and while good to put in your car battery, they confer no benefit to your dragons.

As mentioned above, reptiles also obtain fluids from their food. You can offer veggies to your dragons after first applying a thin layer of water to them and they will obtain much needed fluid as a result of eating the vegetables. Animal foods contain fluids that are passed on to beardies.

In addition to using food as a water vehicle, you can also lightly mist your dragons several times a day with a plant sprayer. For the health of your beardies, purchase a new spray bottle to be used just for this purpose and do not use it for any other. In their arid environment, Bearded Dragons will lap up rainwater as it drips down their heads toward their mouth. Like frogs, dragons love rain and enjoy being sprinkled this way.

WATER DISH TIP

If you are intent on getting your beardie to drink from a water dish, you might try giving your pet a carbonated, lightly perfumed or flavored water. When I offered regular bottled spa water, one of my dragons refused to drink, but when offered water lightly scented with strawberry flavoring, he lapped it up. After a few "fill-ups," I replaced the scented water with plain spa water and this dragon has been drinking from the water dish ever since! Sneaky, eh?

If you are worried about the contents of commercial "designer" waters, make your own by squeezing the juice of a berry into the water. Chilling before serving is optional.

chapter 9

Health Care
for
Bearded Dragons

Because it is illegal to export wild-caught animals from Australia, all Bearded Dragons in the hobbyist or pet trade today are captive-bred. As a result, the lizards tend to be a healthy and hardy species. Lizards that live in the wild acquire  all sorts of bacterial, fungal and parasitic diseases to which they develop immunities. When captured, shipped and kept in captivity, these animals become stressed and their immunity rapidly declines. Hobbyists, in turn, wind up with sick animals, some overtly so.

Nonetheless, beardies can certainly contract a variety of diseases. They can acquire them in large-scale holding and breeding facilities where handlers go from one lizard to another without hand-washing. They may also become ill if such handlers do not take other appropriate precautions, such as removing water or food dishes and then returning them to other tanks without first disinfecting them. Many respiratory infections may be airborne, so beardies can become ill just by being in close proximity to other lizards that may be sick.

When to Visit the Veterinarian

It is important to find a veterinarian with experience treating reptiles when you first obtain your Bearded Dragon. Don't wait until your pet is under the weather to locate a qualified professional. The Association of Reptile and Amphibian Veterinarians (see chapter 12) can help you find a veterinarian in your area. Doctors with no experience with lizards can make an uninformed decision that may cost a lot of money as well as the life of your animal. If the animal is in the early stages of illness and you can see no improvement within a few days of home treatment, it is best to take the beardie in for a medical examination. Because veterinary bills may be quite high, you should ask yourself if you are comfortable paying for treatment that may not even benefit your beardie.

Health Problems Affecting Bearded Dragons

Health problems in Bearded Dragons can be categorized into the same sorts of disorders seen in other animals and people. They include hereditary diseases, nutritional disorders, traumatic injuries, infectious diseases (bacterial, viral, fungal and parasitic), reproductive disorders, neurological disorders and reactions to environmental contaminants and toxins.

HEREDITARY OR GENETIC DISEASES

Hereditary or genetic diseases are problems that Bearded Dragons are born with. They are more commonly found in the offspring of dragons that are close relatives. For example, when one parent is the sibling of the other, it is more likely that a genetic disorder will occur in the children than if the parents are unrelated. To take an extreme and amusing example, if a family of dragons has weak eyesight, and two closely related members are bred with each other, it is possible that your Bearded Dragon will need eyeglasses to see its food.

One class of hereditary diseases involves dragons born with tail and limb deformities, some of which are ultimately lethal. In one recent case, a dragon was born live with one head and two bodies, an unheard of event. It died not long after hatching. As a rule, egg abnormalities such as this result in the birth of either Siamese twins (two fully formed but connected lizards) or one lizard with two heads. Scientists are not certain if such deformities are truly hereditary, if they are based on improper egg husbandry or if they result from a combination of both. A genetic basis for these deformities is supported by the fact that other hatchlings from the same clutch, incubated in just the same way, are perfectly normal.

Tail deformities, such as those shown here, are not uncommon in Bearded Dragons.

Although many reptiles become ill with cancerous diseases and tumors, to date this has not been a problem with Bearded Dragons. However, if there is a genetic basis for the predisposition to such diseases, and immunity to them is diminished by inbreeding, such disorders may be seen in the future as more and more beardeds in the current captive-bred market tend to be related in one way or another. This kind of situation is engendered by the absence of new, foreign or wild-caught stock that would add greater variety to the genetic pool. There appears to be enough unrelated or very distantly related breeding stock available, so this is not likely to occur anytime soon. But unless new stock is made available, there will come a day in the U.S. when every Bearded Dragon is related to every other Bearded Dragon, at least on the species level.

NUTRITIONAL DISORDERS

All reptiles and amphibians are subject to a number of nutritional disorders, including Bearded Dragons.

Calcium and Vitamin D_3 Deficiencies

Calcium and vitamin D_3 deficiencies are very problematic for beardies. Acute calcium deficiency produces convulsive twitching, spasm, the "shakes" and full-blown seizures that can and often do result in death. On a more subtle level, occurring over time, calcium and vitamin D_3 deficiencies result in poor bone growth, brittleness of existing bones and soft bones (e.g. "rubber jaw"). These can result in stunted growth, deformities of long bones and when the jaw is affected, they can in turn affect or prevent feeding. Prevention and treatment of calcium and vitamin D_3 deficiencies involve exposure to direct, unfiltered sunlight for several hours each day, plus the addition of a dietary supplement to the food consisting of calcium carbonate, calcium gluconate and vitamin D_3. Note that a dragon's intake of phosphorus is important. If a part of the beardie's diet, phosphorus should ideally be present in amounts half that of the useable calcium. Phosphorus levels that exceed calcium levels can prevent proper absorption of calcium for bone growth.

> **HOW DO YOU KNOW YOUR BEARDIE IS SICK?**
>
> Sick Bearded Dragons behave like sick puppies, kittens and, yes, even people. They look sick, they act sick and they show symptoms suggestive of the kind of illness that is affecting them. If your dragon is sluggish or won't eat; if it lays flat on the ground (a posture that is normal for sleeping at night but not during daylight when awake); if it doesn't move much or at all—your beardie should be taken to the veterinarian immediately.

It is critical to provide a nutritionally adequate or calcium-supplemented diet, particularly in developing juvenile or baby lizards, as well as adult females being bred. Failure to do so can result in rickets, metabolic bone disease, impaired nervous system transmission and poor eggshell production. Calcium is also important for normal cardiac function in addition to being an integral part of healthy skin, bone, muscle and blood.

Beta-Carotene Deficiency

Color morphs of various dragon species with exceptionally bright coloration are available in the pet trade. Some are known by trademarked names, such as Sandfire Dragons, Golden Dragons and the like. The colors may fade over time, however, if sufficient beta-carotene is not present in the dragon's diet or nutritional supplement. A diet that contains some yellow vegetables, most notably raw carrots, will go far to maintain the morph's special color.

The bright colors of color morphs may fade if the animal does not have sufficient beta-carotene in its diet.

Overfeeding

Another nutritionally related disorder occurs as a result of overfeeding juvenile or newborn Bearded Dragons. These animals will tackle a cricket as large as themselves and attempt to engorge themselves with such a morsel. They will also overeat other types of bugs, such as mealworm or waxworm larvae, if given the opportunity. This can result in partial paralysis of and extension of the hind quarters. This "spastic hind leg extension" was once believed to be a result of calcium deficiency. However, hobbyists and breeders that have conscientiously provided plenty of useable calcium and unfiltered sunlight have observed this condition when overeating occurs. The condition is usually fatal and is the result of pressure from the food bolus on the lower spinal nerves. Do not, therefore, overfeed juvenile dragons, and never feed them large or

Beardies may "look tough" but their little bodies are subject to injury. This dragon suffered a trauma to its tail.

bulky prey items even though they are quite willing to eat them. Small crickets, fed frequently and in moderate amounts, are a much better choice than larger bugs.

TRAUMATIC INJURIES

Bearded Dragons, when housed with other Bearded Dragons, are apt to suffer traumatic injuries as a result of combative or aggressive behavior of one animal against another. Thus it is not unusual for less aggressive members to have toes and tail tips nipped off. One juvenile dragon in my group was bitten on the eye by a cagemate of the same size and age, and nothing could be done to save the eye. Eventually the poor animal succumbed. Separate caging is the key to trauma prevention of this nature in beardeds. Bite injuries should be treated with the use of a disinfectant ointment, such as Betadine. An injury to the eye such as described above was much more difficult to successfully heal.

In addition to injuries inflicted by cagemates, Bearded Dragons can be burned by hot rocks or seared by basking lamps if they cannot escape them when it gets too hot. Burns should be evaluated and treated by a veterinarian, but you can also try any number of over-the-counter burn creams and salves on an emergency basis. If skin is completely burned away (a first-degree burn), professional attention is a necessity. Burns can easily become infected, and death by septicemia is often the result in severe burns that are not properly treated.

INFECTIOUS DISEASES

Infectious diseases are caused by exposure to bacteria, fungi, viruses or parasites. Parasites may either be microscopic (protozoan or unicellular parasites) or large enough to see with the naked eye (metazoan or multicellular parasites). Fungal infections are often profuse enough to see with the unaided eye. The organisms that cause bacterial and viral diseases are so small they cannot be seen without the aid of a microscope but their symptoms are usually easy to spot.

The common feature among all infectious diseases is that they can be transmitted between the environment and the host (in this case your Bearded Dragon is the host) or from one animal to another. On occasion, such diseases can be transmitted from animals to people and vice versa.

Respiratory Infections

Respiratory ailments can be caused by bacteria, viruses and, less frequently, by fungi. Respiratory infections are rare among beardies. When they do occur, they are often the result of improper environmental conditions, including temperatures that are too low, humidity levels that are too high or both. Symptoms include gaping, noisy breathing, puffiness around the throat pouch and mucus discharge from the nostrils and/or mouth. Because such infections are potentially fatal, a trip to the veterinarian is usually required. In the meantime, keep your sick dragon warm (in an enclosure that is 90°F), and at a relatively low humidity.

> **THE RAMIFICATIONS OF HOSTILITY AMONG BEARDIES**
>
> According to Agama International, the aggressive nature of beardies and the resulting injuries make large-scale rearing of clutches in a single enclosure a problem to be reckoned with. Buyers only want perfect specimens, and in order to provide them, such baby dragons need to be housed separately. This is, obviously, more expensive and more laborious than housing and feeding a large number of animals in a communal enclosure. The need to keep beardies in separate cages is one reason that the wholesale cost of baby Bearded Dragons is likely to hover around $30. In contrast, the wholesale price of a baby Green Iguana, which can be communally raised, is usually as low as $3. In any case, Bearded Dragons are definitely worth the extra money—$30 is not all that much to spend on a reptile pet with so much going for it.

Note, however, that gaping may also be the result of overheating, something that should be obvious if you check your enclosure's temperature. Gaping may also be a symptom of lung worms, a parasitic disease. If you are at all uncertain about the cause of your dragon's distress, make an appointment with your veterinarian right away.

Gaping may be a sign of a respiratory infection, a sign of parasitic disease or a sign that your pet is too hot. If you see your beardie gaping and don't know how to respond, get it to the veterinarian as quickly as possible.

FIGHTING INFECTIONS AT HOME

In some cases, you may be able to treat infections in your dragons by increasing the temperature of their basking spot. In nature, reptiles with infections tend to allow themselves to heat up, inducing a fever, if you will, in an apparent effort to subdue or kill off infectious organisms. According to some breeders and hobbyists, this simple home treatment frequently works better than expensive antibiotics.

Gastrointestinal Infections

Gastrointestinal infections are most commonly caused by an overgrowth of bacteria such as *E. coli, Salmonella* sp., *Pseudomonas* sp. and other organisms. Symptoms include loss of appetite, weight loss, listlessness and foul-smelling diarrhea. Lizards do not vomit, and so even if they have symptoms of nausea they cannot relieve themselves in this way. A gastrointestinal infection should be evaluated quickly by a veterinarian who can do a fecal examination. Delay can be fatal, so consider this type of infection a real emergency.

Viral Diseases

Reptiles are subject to contracting viruses, and findings of adenoviruses in Bearded Dragons have been reported. Because antibiotics are ineffective at fighting viral infections, the best treatment is to warm the animal, inducing a fever unfavorable to the virus.

Other lizard viruses known to occur are from the family of poxviruses and papilloma (herpes) virus. Papillomas, or flattened "warts" were discovered in Emerald Lizards, at the base of the tail in females and at the base of the neck in males. The warts were associated with mating bites. As part of the mating ritual, females bite males on the neck and males bite females at the base of the tail. Because Bearded Dragons are also known to bite each other during mating, it is possible that they may develop similar viral infections.

Fungal Diseases

Fungal diseases occur in damp, warm environments and thus are not a known problem in desert and dry land dwelling Bearded Dragons. Some types of cage substrate, such as corncob (which is heavily infused with dormant fungal spores), rapidly vegetate with fungal growth when exposed to dampness and heat. This type of substrate is not recommended for any reptile, especially those that may accidentally ingest it with food matter.

In beardies, the most likely place a fungus may occur would be in a skin abrasion or cut. This should be rapidly treated with an antifungal, such as Lotrimin, or by a veterinarian using an antifungal agent or antibiotic known to fight fungal conditions.

Parasitic Infections

Parasites are classified by their physical relationship with their host. Parasites that reside on the outside of a host, such as mites, fleas, ticks or maggots, are known as ectoparasites. Those that live inside a host are called endoparasites. Reptiles are susceptible to and may harbor both types of parasites. There are many methods of ridding your beardies of parasites, and not all of them can be addressed here. As a rule, it is best to seek professional help when your lizard has a parasitic infection.

Many hobbyists, however, effectively use home treatments on their animals. This is only a good solution if you are confident that you can diagnose the problem properly and treat it competently.

Ectoparasites   Hobbyists treat ectoparasites with No-Pest Strips placed not far from (but not in or on top of) cages, hoping to attract mites and ticks off the animal and killing them with the vapors. Other methods include bathing the animal in dilute solutions of Betadine and water (colored like weak tea) or even in a solution of Listerine and water (tinged light gold). Some hobbyists use a topical solution of the antiparasite drug Ivermectin, which is available over-the-counter in feed stores. Recommended doses of the latter drug

On occasion, the stress of being shipped will cause a latent case of cryptosporidosis to emerge as a serious illness.

are provided for huge animals—horses and cows. It should be diluted for use as a topical ointment at a ratio of 0.5ml of the drug to a quart of water. Using the drug internally can be very dangerous to your animal so this should be left up to a knowledgeable veterinarian.

Endoparasites   One of the most prevalent endoparasites found in Bearded Dragons in the U.S. is a coccidian known as *Cryptosporidium*, which causes a disease called crypto-sporidosis or "crypto" for short. In recent years, crypto has been showing up in some municipal water supplies, and it is not clear whether it is resistant to conventional chlorination procedures or if the water supplies in question are being adequately treated. The organism is too small to be captured by many home and industrial water filtering systems. Boiling tap water or providing sterile bottled water are alternatives in areas where crypto is known to be present in water supplies.

Veterinary researchers have reported crypto showing up in increasing numbers among captive reptiles, often wiping out entire collections before its presence was detected and could be properly treated. Breeders may start out shipping apparently healthy animals that then become stressed by the rigors of transport and excessive handling. By the time they reach the home hobbyist's cage, their previously undetectable infection may be a full-blown case. Such animals need to be diagnosed and treated by a veterinarian, but if the infection is overwhelming the prognosis may not be good.

Another endoparasite found in Bearded Dragons is *Microspora* sp., which causes microsporiodosis. Until recently, *Microspora* sp. was believed to predominantly infect fish, most notably ornamental tropical fish. It has rarely been identified in amphibians and some reptiles, and only quite recently in beardies. Tropical fish hobbyists have much experience with this parasite and admit there is no definitive treatment for it. In fish, the organism not only occupies the gastrointestinal tract, but it also attacks internal organs and eventually kills its host. In view of the appearance of this organism in Bearded Dragons, it may be unwise to attempt feeding them feeder tropical fish that you might purchase in a pet shop. Microspora are difficult for Bearded Dragons or any animal they infect for two very important reasons: They have a direct life cycle (they don't need an intermediate host to reproduce), and

KEEP YOURSELF HEALTHY, TOO

One of the most common (and normal) intestinal bacteria in reptiles is Salmonella. Salmonella, along with a variety of other microorganisms, are known as zoonotic diseases or zoonoses. Zoonoses are infections that can be transmitted from animals to humans. They are entirely preventable by thorough handwashing for thirty seconds with hot water and disinfectant soap after handling any reptiles. In addition, you must be careful when cleaning your reptile's cage furnishings and water bowls in sinks used for human activities, such as kitchen sinks and bathroom sinks. Be sure to remove all articles used for human purposes from the sink area, and to thoroughly disinfect sinks and countertops before returning to them. If possible, devote one sink in your home for beardie use only.

Zoonoses are especially dangerous to people immuno-compromised because of a disease, such as HIV, or a medication or other treatment they are receiving. Children under 8 years old are liable to suffer more seriously from zoonotic infection than adults. Unborn fetuses are also at high risk, and accordingly, moms-to-be must be meticulous when handling reptiles or cleaning cages.

they form highly resistant spores that can exist up to a year or more in the environment, even in the absence of a host. Some researchers believe the source of infection in beardies may, indeed, be ingestion of such spores, which are liable to be anywhere.

A coccidian commonly found in Bearded Dragons is *Isospora amphiboluri*. This organism, in fact, is even named after an earlier generic name for beardies—*Amphibolurus*. These parasites are so common that they may be considered commensals, or microorganisms that exist at the expense of the host but do not harm it (or they lose their free ride). However, it is not a good idea to leave them untreated in captives that may have depressed immune systems as a result of inadequate conditions or the mere stress of captivity. In beardies of questionable health, these organisms can rapidly reproduce and reach excessive and definitely harmful levels. Coccidia invade the mucus lining of the intestinal tract, which they feed on in order to grow and reproduce.

Isopora is a parasite commonly found in beardies. Even the baby dragon you buy may be infected. Your veterinarian can help you eliminate this problem.

In heavy infestations, they can cause your dragon stomach pain, diarrhea and nutritional malabsorption. Moreover, in connection with the diarrhea, dragons lose fluids (which they can ill, afford, given the difficulty hobbyists have in getting them to accept fluids at all). Needless to say, this situation can easily lead to your lizard's death.

Because it is not known where or how *Isospora* is contracted, getting and isolating a newborn beardie is no guarantee it will be *Isospora* free. Some veterinarians have even suggested it may be passed to unborn beardies before the embryo is shelled or it may even migrate through the shell wall. There are only two drugs available that may work to combat Isospora: sulfamethoxine and trimethoprim-sulfa. Sulfa drugs should only be used if coccidiosis is a confirmed diagnosis, according to veterinary authorities on these parasites. Because the bug will come back as fast as you eliminate it, you also have to change cages frequently during the treatment cycle in order to prevent reinfection. Infected animals should actually have two cages: one for housing the dragon and one to be sterilized. The animal should be moved back and forth into a freshly cleaned cage frequently. You may have to keep this process up for as long as six weeks before your veterinarian gives your beardie a clean bill of health. It is best to keep the cages free of accessories—everything in the cage will also have to be sterilized repeatedly.

Another dangerous parasite, which is rare in the U.S. water supply (but not in some foreign locales where sewerage and sanitation may be poor to nonexistent), is *Entamoeba invadens*. This organism causes amoebic dysentery, which is not very different from the same condition in humans caused by *Entamoeba histolytica*. The parasite causes gastroenteritis marked by bloody diarrhea, failure or unwillingness to eat (anorexia) and often culminates in death. It can be treated by a veterinarian once the diagnosis is established.

Finally, beardies are frequently afflicted by infestations of pinworms, also known as oxyurids. Generally, pinworms are less harmful and easier to treat than other parasites. However, they can quickly reach burdensome levels. Your veterinarian can check for pinworms by examining your beardie's feces and treat them with a short course of the drug Panacur.

REPRODUCTIVE DISORDERS

The most common reproductive disorder seen in adult dragons is egg-binding or dystocia. There are many possible causes for egg-binding, including poor diet and calcium deficiency, generalized weakness or debilitation, low weight, obesity and other illness. If your dragon cannot find or select a suitable site to dig a nest, the stress can also result in egg-binding. If the cause is anything but the last (which you can rectify by quickly establishing a deep soil-based substrate for the dragon to build her nest), then a trip to the veterinarian is in order as soon as the problem is recognized. A drug known as pitocin or vasotocin can be administered, which would induce contractions that lead to the expulsion of the eggs. Egg-binding can be fatal if not quickly relieved. If the lizard does not respond to the drug, surgery to remove the eggs may be necessary.

EXPECTANT BEARDIES NEED SPECIAL CARE

Poor nutrition can prevent successful reproduction. If your female lays small, shriveled-up eggs or slugs, which are shell-less, semisolid or solid balls of yellowish yolk plugs, your female may be suffering from a dietary deficiency rendering it incapable of nourishing and shelling its eggs prior to expulsion.

Observe a gravid female carefully. If your beardie is egg-bound, you want to be aware of it as soon as the problem arises. If the animal stops eating for several days and is constantly rooting about looking to deposit her eggs but is either unable to do so or is unable to select a suitable site (even if provided), then you can be reasonably certain your dragon is in trouble.

The stress of having no suitable nesting site can cause a Bearded Dragon to become egg-bound. A deep, soil-based substrate is a must if your beardie is expecting.

NEUROLOGICAL DISORDERS

Most neurological problems seen in Bearded Dragons can be traced to dietary deficiency. It is particularly important to be sure that your dragons get enough calcium, as a diet lacking in calcium may lead to neurological symptoms, such as spasm, twitching and seizures.

Lizard owners should also be on the lookout for Inclusion Body Disease (IBD), an unidentified virus that attacks the brain and spinal tissues. Although infection with this disease has not yet been found in beardies, it has been well-documented in snakes and is believed to have spread to captive lizards. Symptoms include "star-gazing" (an upward tilt of the head) and other strange postures maintained over long time periods. There is no known cure for this condition, but early recognition is essential to limit the spread of the disease in collections. Affected animals should be quarantined, preferably in separate rooms. After coming into contact with an affected animal, keepers should thoroughly disinfect their hands and even change their clothing before having contact with healthy lizards.

A healthy Bearded Dragon is active and alert. If your pet is listless or refuses food, make an appointment with your veterinarian right away.

ENVIRONMENTAL CONTAMINANTS AND TOXINS

A wide variety of common household substances can be toxic to amphibians and reptiles, including Bearded Dragons. These include glass cleaners and other cleaning compounds, insecticides, chemical fertilizers, weed killers and perhaps even the disinfectant soap that you use to clean your animal's food or water dishes. Such substances need to be kept far away from your dragons. When cleaning food and water dishes, be sure to thoroughly rinse away any soapy or disinfectant residue. Be especially careful about using insecticide sprays or other volatile compounds around your beardies—the molecules of these sprays enter the air freely and can be inhaled by your lizard. Exposure to chemicals can result in neurological problems, with a variety of symptoms, such as seizures, twitching, the star-gazing symptom and other bizarre and unusual signs.

If you include live plants in your enclosure, it is necessary to remember that beardies like to eat leaves and the leaves of many ornamental houseplants may be toxic to any animals that ingest them. In addition, store-bought plants may have been sprayed with pesticides. Be sure to wash these plants thoroughly before placing them in your beardie's cage. Artificial plants are a far better choice.

chapter 10

Breeding

Bearded
Dragons

According to some long-term professional breeders of beardies, the huge numbers of these lizards being bred in captivity outside of Australia may soon make them the most popular species of pet lizard. In spite of a paucity of field research on beardies in the  wild, their captive husbandry and breeding is now among the best understood and managed of any agamid lizard.

Sexing

The first consideration for any would-be breeder is to be sure to place a male and female together for the purposes of mating. Two males may soon start fighting and hurt each other before they can be separated. Even males and females play rough, with males biting females in the neck and females taking nips at the toes and tail tips of the males.

There are a number of ways to distinguish males from females. Sexual dimorphism is the phrase used to describe differences in the outward appearance of males and females of a particular species. In Bearded Dragons, males and females display no obvious differences in color, structure or anatomy. However, males have larger heads than females and bob their heads more slowly. Females tend to be larger in the abdominal girth than males. The gular or "beard" region tends to be darker in males than in females.

One way to distinguish a male from a female is by comparing the size of the heads. The male head (top) is a good deal wider than that of the female.

Males have larger, more prominent pores around their anal and femoral region. The femoral pores of Bearded Dragons are not located in the middle of a scale but actually between two scales. If taught how to do so, one can also evert the hemipenes, thus identifying the specimen in hand as a male. But the best way to separate the sexes is by looking at the hemipenile bulges, which occur on each side of the base of the tail. To make these bulges appear, place an 8-month to 1-year-old or older (6- to 8-inch snout/vent length) lizard flat on its stomach and, holding it flat with one hand along the back, use the other hand to gently lift the tail so it is standing almost straight up at a 90 degree angle. Be careful not to bend back the tail too far or you might snap a vertebra at the base of the tail. If you see two bulges on either side of the tail base, then you have a male. If you see one bulge more centrally located, the beardie is a female.

Getting to Know You

Once you have an identified pair, introduce them to each other. Think of this as a beardie blind date. Place them together in a new and very large enclosure (at least 5 to 6 feet in length and 2 feet wide). Be sure there is a high branch for the dominant male and lower basking sites for the female. Establish separate

feeding areas. Mating will be preceded by frequent head bobbing and arm waving, as well as nipping and biting. If encounters become too aggressive and blood is drawn, it is a good idea to place the pair in separate quarters. Rearrange the setup in the breeding enclosure and rein-troduce the lizards to the cage. If you have more than one female, you may want to move two or three females in with a single male. He will mate with all the females, pro-duce a much larger yield of offspring during this inter-lude and the kind of aggressiveness seen between a sin-gle female and male placed together is less likely to occur. Even in this situation, however, fighting is not unusual and is to be expected during mating attempts.

The dark beard of this dragon is a sign that it is a male.

Conditioning and Nutrition

Before mating is attempted, it is essential that you house males and females separately and keep them well fed on a varied diet. For two or three weeks before mat-ing, add a triple calcium supplement to the female's diet on a daily basis.

A number of factors influence breeding, including cycles of light and darkness and temperature. In the pre-mating period, hours of light should be lowered to ten per day and darkness should occupy fourteen hours per day. Daytime temperatures should be allowed to drop to 75° to 85°F and to as low as 55° to 60°F at night. These conditions closely simulate the Australian spring, which is when pre-breeding cycling occurs in these lizards. Spermatogenesis in males occurs from autumn over the winter to early spring in Australia; mating occurs in the spring, and ovulation occurs shortly thereafter. Although the seasons in Australia are reversed with those in the United States, for your purposes, this is irrelevant. You are controlling conditions that simulate the seasons during which these events take place. In the U.S., the reduced light period and temperatures may well begin the first two weeks of December and be allowed to occur through mid-February. By then, you should increase the light period to fourteen hours and temperatures should be returned to 85°F.

An indoor breeding pen should have different levels of basking sites and an accessible nesting site.

Within a month of returning to normal conditions, breeding behavior will occur. At this time, both beardies should be fed a calcium-supplemented meal once daily and a second, unsupplemented meal, if they will eat it. Females should be fed a varied, supplemented diet until the end of the summer, consisting of equal parts animal and vegetable matter at different servings.

Egg Laying

Bearded Dragons are hole or burrow nesters. They will not lay their eggs until they have dug what they consider to be a suitable burrow in which to deposit them. Failure to provide the correct substrate for this purpose may stress the female and subject her to egg binding. If the substrate is too "flaky," any hole the dragon creates is apt to close up as she digs; if the substrate is too hard or compact, she will be unable to make any headway in it. A combination of sterile potting soil and sand is recommended.

A Bearded Dragon digs a hole in which to lay her eggs.

Although this may sound silly, you can lay out a mixture in a small area and test it yourself by shoveling into it. If the hole you shovel out remains fairly well intact, it is suitable for Bearded Dragon nesting. You can leave these man-made burrows in the enclosure and introduce the female to them so she gets the idea. The time to do this is when you see her furiously rooting around for a place to dig in her normal quarters. According to commercial breeders, some females will use a man-made burrow as a starting point, dig it out the rest of the way and deposit her eggs therein. You should provide a heap of soil at least 8 to 12 inches deep and at least 2 to 3 square feet in area.

If you allow your females to dig into an outdoor enclosure with a natural floor, be sure to flag the spot after she closes the nest so that you can remove the eggs later for

BREEDING FOR PROFIT?

Beardies are fecund and, at a wholesale price of about $30 per hatchling, each female can generate from $600 to slightly over $1,000 per season in income for the dedicated home breeder. Babies may be sold in quantity to mail-order dealers or marketed to pet shops in the breeder's region. They can also be sold by ads in the local newspaper pet classified section, the classified section of reptile hobby magazines, over the Internet or taken to reptile swap meets or expos. You are not likely to get rich breeding and selling Bearded Dragons, but the small amount of extra income you can make by doing so helps your hobby pay for itself. Note that if you actually make a profit selling your dragons, you may have to include your earnings in your taxable income. Check with your tax adviser for detailed information.

artificial incubation. Leaving incubation to chance in an outdoor situation may greatly decrease hatching success rate.

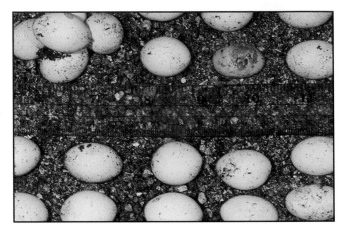

These eggs are being incubated on a bed of moistened vermiculite. In a given clutch, some of the eggs may not survive. Note the egg that has turned pink— this is a sign that the egg is failing.

Clutch Size

The number of eggs laid by any one female Bearded Dragon is highly variable. Clutch size depends on a number of factors including the female's age, physical condition and the extent of previous breeding. Larger females between the ages of 2 to 5 years may produce thirty to fifty eggs per clutch. Smaller females may produce as many as fifty fertile eggs per season in two or three different clutches.

Incubating Bearded Dragon Eggs

After your female has dug her nest and deposited her eggs, remove her from the enclosure and carefully uncover the eggs. Be careful not to rotate or turn the eggs upside down. Carefully separate and place each egg in a plastic shoebox, large plastic sweater box or lidded plastic food dish. The bottom of the container should hold a bed consisting of a 2-inch layer of vermiculite and water. The bed should be composed of equal amounts of vermiculite and water by weight: 8 ounces of vermiculite and 8 ounces of water by weight (not volume). (Although some breeders indicate that perlite may be used in lieu of vermiculite, it was recently discovered that perlite can emit substances noxious to eggs and can cause either death of the embryo or birth defects in hatchlings. Vermiculite is a better choice for successful breeding.)

About one-half to two-thirds of the egg should be buried in the bed with the rest of the egg left exposed on top. Cardboard or wood containers are not recommended, as they will absorb the moisture from the substrate. Place a lid over the container. The lid should have predrilled or punched-out airholes, as should the upper sides of the container. Once the eggs are placed, they should not be moved or turned. There are now several methods you can use to incubate your eggs.

You can set up a well-ventilated, temperature-controlled incubator, large enough to accommodate your boxes full of eggs; you can keep them in a place in the house where temperatures approximate those of an incubator (without the benefit of an incubator); or you can simply place the eggs in a dark, well-ventilated spot and

In a large outdoor enclosure, make sure to mark the spot where the nest was closed.

allow them to incubate at room temperature. The warm environment of the first two options will cause the eggs to hatch more quickly than if you allow them to incubate at room temperature.

If you are going to establish an incubator with increased heat, it is important to keep that temperature between 83° and 85°F through thermostatic adjustment. Novice breeders have learned the hard way that incubators can overheat and kill their eggs, so it is important to monitor and adjust the thermostat over a twelve-hour period prior to introducing the eggs. If your incubation period occurs during the warmer months, remember to keep your incubator in a room cooler than that of the incubator temperature. If the room temperature rises to 90°F or more, a thermostatically set temperature of 85°F would be easily surpassed, and you risk damaging or killing your eggs from overheating.

At higher temperatures, humidity in the vermiculite is apt to evaporate. You can help prevent this by placing a container of water in the incubator to maintain humidity levels. Check the vermiculite daily to make sure it is as damp as it was when first set up, and refill your water container as necessary. If the vermiculite needs to be moistened, use a plant sprayer to mist both the eggs and the substrate. Fertile eggs absorb water from their environment and increase in size as a result.

At about 85°F, the following incubator hatching times have been recorded:

Eastern Bearded Dragon, *Pogona barbata*—seventy to eighty days

Inland Bearded Dragon, *Pogona vitticeps*—fifty-five to seventy-five days

Lawson's Dragon, *Pogona henrylawsoni*—forty-five to fifty-five days

---

LEAVE OUTDOOR HATCHING TO THE EXPERTS

Breeders who breed beardies outdoors or in greenhouses where spring and summer temperatures are appropriate often leave their eggs in the nest and allow them to hatch naturally. Because you have little control over temperature and humidity in such a situation, there is no telling what your success rate and time-to-hatching will be. This is dangerous because some hatchlings may not be able to escape either the egg or, if they get that far, then may be unable to escape the nest.

Eggs incubated at cooler temperatures will take longer to hatch.

Hatching Eggs

Usually, eggs hatch over a twenty-four- to seventy-two-hour period. Eggs ready to hatch will collapse or become indented. As a rule, hatching dragons will slit open the egg and release themselves by means of an "egg tooth" located just under the snout on the upper jaw. The egg tooth is lost shortly after hatching.

After most of the eggs have hatched, some collapsed, but unhatched eggs may remain. The baby dragons inside may be too weak to release themselves, or may have an insufficiently developed egg tooth. You may want to assist by using a tiny pair of cuticle scissors or a small scalpel blade. Great care must be taken to cut a slit only in the egg shell and avoid injuring the infant dragon inside. The slit can be between ¼ and ⅓ inch in length, running along the long axis of the top of the egg. Once you make the slit, allow the baby dragon to emerge by itself; don't attempt to pull it from the egg. A large yolk sac may remain and the lizard may not yet be ready to breathe air. Pulling it from the egg after slicing the shell can cause the baby to die. It will emerge spontaneously when it is ready.

A clutch of eggs will usually hatch over the course of one to three days.

Baby Dragons

Baby Bearded Dragons measure about 3 to 4 inches including the tail, depending on the species; body size is usually no more than 1.5 inches and birth weights range from 1.5 to 3.5 grams.

As a rule, few members of a given clutch will be born with birth defects. However, you should be aware that babies can be born with any of the following abnormalities:

- spinal curvature or twisting
- corkscrew spiraling of the tail
- dome-head where the top of the head appears enlarged or puffed-out
- leg abnormalities, including limbs that are folded in or over

- spindly and weak limbs

- dwarfism or failure to grow

These defects may be genetic or the result of nutritional deficits in the laying female. Eggs that are provided inadequate temperature and humidity conditions or that are exposed to toxins may also result in birth defects.

They're so cute!

Nonetheless, there is a large and growing cadre of Bearded Dragon breeders, resulting in the annual production of more than 100,000 of these unique and unusually calm pet reptiles. It is fair to say that no other lizard or reptile has been so easily and successfully bred in such a short period of time as beardies. And their popularity is sure to grow over the years, as wild-caught reptiles become increasingly more difficult to obtain.

part four

Beyond
the
Basics

chapter 11

Bearded Dragons— An Australian Perspective

Australian herpetologist Ray Hoser has written a fascinating article concerning the Bearded Dragon from a down under viewpoint. Ironically, more is known about Bearded Dragons outside Australia than within the country, and Hoser laments that the causes of this are Australia's draconian (no pun intended) wildlife restrictions. According to Hoser, Bearded Dragons are not in need of conservation where most populations and species are concerned. They are under no threat of extinction or extirpation and are relatively common. Tens of thousands of beardies are killed accidentally on the roads every year by motorists. Even areas of degraded or spoiled habitat, as well as habitat modified for human use, contain large numbers of this plucky lizard. Licensing laws in Australia have not protected a single population of these lizards, nor are they ever likely to, according to Hoser. On the other hand, they have legally prevented many Australians from keeping and studying these lizards. An example of the nature

110

of these laws occurred a few years ago when a small schoolchild was arrested by authorities for cooping up some tadpoles to observe for science class.

If any reptiles are to be legally exported from Australia, it makes sense that the number one draft choice should be Bearded Dragons. The fact that tens of thousands die on the country's highways has had no impact on their numbers in the wild, and captive breeding programs of this easy to breed lizard, set up both within the country as well as those already taking place overseas, would keep wild-caught numbers to a minimum. In any case, the numbers permitted for captivity or export could still be regulated by authorities if it were legal to do so.

Australia lags far behind in the captive care and husbandry of one of its own most populous native lizards. The reasons for this include permitting laws that make it difficult or impossible to legally own Bearded Dragons (why risk prison for a lizard?) and the abundance of these animals in the wild, making them less desirable or interesting to keepers. According to Hoser, Australian herpetologists have added to their knowledge of captive care of Bearded Dragons from publications emanating from the U.S. and Europe, a truly ironic situation.

Wild beardies are abundant in Australia, where rigid permitting laws make keeping these lizards onerous.

While all hobbyists agree that the collection of wild-caught specimens should be minimized or eliminated by proliferation of captive-bred animals, Aussie herpetologists admit that at present and for the foreseeable future, beardies are no longer in danger. Their greatest threats are automobiles (roadkill), natural predators and encroachment or spoilage of habitat by humans. Even in the last case, populations of these dragons have managed to survive, side by side with humans, and in no apparent distress. Effective, unnatural predators, such as feral dogs, foxes and cats, have not managed to decimate Bearded Dragon populations. According to Hoser, it is likely that the toll taken by feral or unnatural predators roughly equals that taken by natural predators displaced by feral ones. Thus, the net effect on the Bearded Dragon population is zero.

chapter 12

Resources

Breeder/Dealer Directory

(Note: by including the name of a Bearded Dragon breeder/dealer herein, neither the author nor publisher accepts any responsibility for any commercial dealings between a listed dealer and buyer of Bearded Dragons. This list is for informational purposes only and no endorsement of any companies or individuals listed herein is implied or warranted.)

ALABAMA

CB Reptiles
P.O. Box 161
Maylene, AL 35114
(205) 669-1345
Web site: http://www.herp.com/cbrep/cbrep.html

Dragon's Lair
165 Asberry Rd.
Montevallo, AL 35115
(205) 665-2722

ARIZONA

Atomic Lizard Ranch
(Collette or Paul)
P.O. Box 5644
Bisbee, AZ 85603
(520) 432-9161
E-mail: atomic@theriver.com

Creative Alternatives
(602) 439-1030
E-mail: CreativeAlternatives@NetValue.net
Web site: http://www.creativealternatives.com

CALIFORNIA

Dragon's Den Herpetoculture
P.O. Box 1116
Goleta, CA 93116
Web site: http://www.spydercide.com/lizards

Lima's Exotic Reptiles
P.O. Box 6496
Woodland Hills, CA 91365
(818) 703-1112
E-mail: limasherp@aol.com

Sandfire Dragon Ranch
Bob Mailloux
P.O. Box 665
Bonsall, CA 92003
(760) 726-4878
E-mail: sandfire@compuserve.com
Web site: http://www.thevivarium.com/sandfire.html

Tracy's Ark
(818) 848-5113
E-mail: tracysark@netmeister.net
Web site: http://www.netmeister.net/tracysark

FLORIDA

Paul and Sue Bradshaw
(561) 288-4524

Dan Elliott
5718 12th Ave. S.
Gulfport, FL 33707
(727) 381-4219
E-mail: DanElliott@bigfoot.com

Carl and Janet Fuhri
Dragon's Glade
24576 Amarillo St.
Bonita Springs, FL 34135
(941) 992-5679
E-mail: fuhri@gate.net.com
Web site: www.gate.net/~furhi

Herp Hobby Shop
Oldsmar, FL
(813) 789-5336

Gene Kohlen
99 South Tyler St.
Beverly Hills, FL 34465
(352) 746-0649

Bill and Kathy Love
Blue Chameleon Ventures
P.O. Box 643
Alva, FL 33920
(941) 728-2390
E-mail: blove@cyberstreet.com
Web site: www.cyberstreet.com/loveherp

Rob MacInnes
Glades Herp, Inc.
5207 Palm Beach Blvd.
Ft. Myers, FL 33905
(941) 693-1077
E-mail: gherp@cyberstreet.com
Web site: http://207.30.59.98/herp

Weis Reptiles
Rte 4, Box 468
Tallahassee, FL 32304
(904) 574-1037
E-mail: weisrep@atL.mindspring.com
Web site: http://www.weisreptiles.com

LOUISIANA

Jon Klarsfeld
New Orleans, LA
(504) 269-9986

MICHIGAN

Kathryn Tosney
Ann Arbor, MI
(734) 663-9479
E-mail: ktosney@umich.edu

NEW HAMPSHIRE

New England Reptile Distributors
26 Chandler Ave., #14
Plaistow, NH 03865
(603) 382-6321
Web site: http://www.NewEnglandReptile.com

NEW JERSEY

Tony DiPaolo
Englishtown, NJ
(732) 446-7168

NEW YORK

Al Swanson
P.O. Box 90064
Staten Island, NY 10309
(718) 317-8382

NORTH CAROLINA

Exotic Lizard Ranch
3800-B W. Vernon Ave.
Kinston, NC 28504
(919) 523-7596

PENNSYLVANIA

Serpent's Den
Rte. 209
Milford, PA 18337
(717) 296-5877

Dragon Lady Reptiles
Ft. Davis, TX
(915) 426-3848

Organizations

You should join your local herpetological society. Groups are widespread throughout the U.S. and abroad. For a listing of these, consult: *A Guide to North American Herpetology.*

Internet Resources

In addition to the breeders/dealers who have Web sites or e-mail addresses listed above, the following Internet resources are available to Bearded Dragon hobbyists.

POGONA MAILING LIST OR LISTSERV

A listserv or mailing list is an e-mail forum where questions, responses or general statements on a particular subject are automatically circulated to a group of many people. The following details concern the Pogona mailing list.

This list is dedicated to the discussion of Bearded Dragons (Pogona sp.). Posts should be reasonably related to the topic. Subscribers should adhere to general "netiquette" principles. Flames (posts that are inflammatory or highly critical) and trolls (posts that seek to incite inflammatory of critical remarks) will not be tolerated.

To subscribe to the Pogona list, send an e-mail message addressed to:

pogona-request@lists.best.com

In the body of the message, write just one word:

subsingle

To unsubscribe or sign-off the mailing list, send an e-mail message addressed to:

pogona-request@lists.best.com

In the body of the message, write just one word:

unsubscribe

There is also a digest version of the Pogona list that compiles a batch of posts and sends them to you all at one time at irregular frequencies. To subscribe to the digest version of the pogona list, send an e-mail message as above to:

pogona-request@lists.best.com

And in the body of the message, write one word:

subscribe

You will automatically receive a welcome message with details and instructions about the list. It is a good idea to file this message on your computer for future reference. And once you've done the above, you will also start to receive messages about Bearded Dragons and you will also be able to ask questions, make comments or statements or answer questions yourself. When you hit the automatic reply button, your answer will go to the individual who posted the question or comment. If you want to share your response with all the other list members, either hit the "Reply to All" button or insert the e-mail address of the list as a cc or bcc in your e-mail header. This address is: pogona@lists.best.com

To post a new message directly to the list, be it a question, comment or response to a discussion already in progress, enter a short description of the subject in the subject or re: section of your e-mail header and address the message to:

pogona@lists.best.com

The moderator of the Pogona list is Alta Brewer. If you have any specific questions or problems getting subscribed or posting, you can contact Alta by private e-mail at:

altab@netwizards.net

THE WORLD WIDE WEB

You can find documents and Web sites devoted to Bearded Dragons on the World Wide Web (www). Some of the sites you may consider worth visiting have been compiled here.

Colorado Herpetological Society's Web site—Bearded Dragon Care Sheets:

> http://www.goho.org/~coloherp/careshts/bearded-eds.html

Japanese Bearded Dragon Web site (English version available):

> http://www.hemi.com/~kiyo8723/dragon/indexe.html

Xena—The Warrior Lizard (Bearded Dragon):

> http://www.olywa.net/diablo/lizard/mike.html

Bearded Dragons—On-Line

> http://www.3rdimension.com/Dragon/

El Dorado Dragon Ranch

> http://www.ns.net/~pweber/dragons/index.html

Karnivor's Bearded Dragon Care and Information Web site

> http://members.xoom.com/Karnivor/beardies.htm

Peter Weis's Bearded Dragon Page

> http://www.echonyc.com/~gecko/herps/lizards/bearded.html

Sonny's Bearded Dragon Page

http://members.tripod.com/~bassdrop/index.html

Surfing the Web will reveal many more Bearded Dragon Web sites. Entering the word "pogona" into a search engine, such as AltaVista, will return a trove of Web sites on Bearded Dragons that will keep you busy long into the night.

Veterinary Services for Bearded Dragons

To find a veterinarian near you who is experienced with reptiles, contact:

Wilbur B. Amand, DVM
Association of Reptilian and Amphibian
Veterinarians (ARAV)
P.O. Box 605
One Smithbridge Rd.
Chester Heights, PA 19017

Membership in the ARAV is open to anyone (not just veterinarians) interested in the health care of reptiles. It includes a quarterly bulletin and admission to local chapter meetings. Dr. Amand regrets he is unable to field telephone queries, so it is necessary to write him for information.

Live Food Dealers

The following firms will mail order quantities of feeder insects and supplies. Contact them for their latest price lists and terms directly:

Arbico
(800) 827-2847

Armstrong's Cricket Farm
P.O. Box 745
Glennville, GA 30427
(800) 345-8778

Armstrong's Cricket Farm (Louisiana)
P.O. Box 125
West Monroe, LA 71294
(800) 345-8778

Bassetts Cricket Ranch, Inc.
(800) 634-2445

Butterworms
EXPOBAIT
8030 Deerfield St.
San Diego, CA 92120
(619) 582-8862

Drosophila (Flightless Fruitflies)
(800) 545-2303
Web site: http://vpro.net/drosophila

Fluker Farms
1333 Plantation Ave.
Port Allen, LA 70767
(504) 343-7035

Ghann's Cricket Farm, Inc.
P.O. Box 211840
August, GA 30917
(800) 476-2248

Grubco
P.O. Box 15001
Hamilton, OH 45015
(800) 222-3563
Web site: http://www.herp.com/grubco

Jurassic Snacks
(888) 427-6225
E-mail: jurassic@lr.net
Web site: http://www.jurassicsnacks.com

Milbrook Cricket Farm
(800) 654-3506

M&S Reptilien
AlbstraBe 18/1+2
D-78056 VS-Weigheim
Germany
0-7425/31447

Nature's Way
(800) 318-2611
Web site: http://www.herp.com/nature

Powers Science Materials
3875 Franklin Rd.
Jackson, MI 49203
(517) 764-5929
Web site: http://www.adveworld.com/feedermice

Rainbow Mealworms
126 E. Spruce St. (P.O. Box 4907)
Compton, CA 90224
(800) 777-9676

Sunshine Mealworms
7263 Gallon House Rd.
Silverton, OR 97381
(800) 322-1100

Timberline
(800) 423-2248
E-mail: livefood@timberlinefisheries.com
Web site: http://www.timberlinefisheries.com

Top Hat Cricket Farm, Inc.
1919 Forest Dr.
Kalamazoo, MI 49002
(800) 638-2555

Triple R Cricket Ranch
31585 Road 68
Visalia, CA 93291
(800) 238-2808

Nutritional Supplements and Non-Live Foods

Calanpro Laboratories
California Animal Products
P.O. Box 1419
Alpine, CA 91903

Dragon Pet KM Mineral Supplement
(303) 494-4443

Fluker Laboratories
(504) 343-7035

Miner-All
Sticky Tongue Farms
26900 Newport Rd.
Menifree, CA 92584
(909) 672-3876
E-mail: stckyfrm@pe.net
Web site: http://www.biohaven.com/bus/stf

Nekton-USA
14405 60th St. N.
Clearwater, FL 34620

Rep-Cal Research Labs
P.O. Box 727
Los Gatos, CA 95031
(408) 356-4289
(800) 406-6446
Web site: http://www.repcal.com

T-Rex Products
1124 Bay Blvd.
Chula Vista, CA 919
(619) 424-1050
Web site: http://www.t-rexproducts.com

Tetra-Terrafauna
3001 Commerce St.
Blacksburg, VA 24060
(540) 951-5400
Web site: http://www.tetra-fish.com

The above listings are primarily of manufacturers, many of which do not sell directly to the public. If you call, ask them for literature on their reptile nutritional and non-live food products, particularly calcium supplements and Bearded Dragon diets. They can also refer you to local or mail-order dealers that carry their products.

Thermoregulatory, Full Spectrum Lighting, Heating and Reptile Egg Incubation Equipment

Black Jungle Terrarium Supply
P.O. Box 93895
Las Vegas, NV 89193
(702) 242-0220

Energy Savers Unlimited, Inc.
Web site: http://www.esuweb.com

Helix Controls
12225 World Trade Dr. (Suite C)
San Diego, CA 92128
(619) 674-7480
Web site: http://www.herp.com/helix/helix.html

J.S. Technologies
Habi-Temp
P.O. Box 12420
La Crescenta, CA 91224
(818) 353-1577
E-mail: jstech@earthlink.net

Kane Reptile Heat Mats
P.O. Box 774
Des Moines, IA 50303
(515) 262-3001
E-mail: kanemfg@worldnet.att.net

Lyon Electric Co. Inc.
Reptile Incubation Systems
2765 Main St.
Chula Vista, CA 91911
(619) 585-9900

Pro Products
36 Split Rock Rd.
Mahopac, NY 10541
(914) 628-8960
Web site: http://www.pro-products.com

Randall Burkey Co., Inc.
Incubators
117 Industrial Dr.
Boerne, TX 78006
(800) 531-1097

Reptronics
170 Creek Rd.
Bangor, PA 18013
(610) 588-6011

Vita-Lite
c/o Duro-Lite Lamps
9 Law Dr.
Fairfield, NJ 07004
(888) 738-8482

ZooMed Laboratories, Inc.
3199 McMillan
San Luis Obispo, CA 93401
(805) 542-9988
E-mail: zoomed@zoomed.com
Web site: http://www.zoomed.com

Further Reading and References

Cogger, Harold. *Reptiles and Amphibians of Australia,* 5th ed. Ithaca, NY: Comstock-Cornell University Press, 1994.

DeVosjoli, P. and R. Mailloux. *General Care and Maintenance of Bearded Dragons.* Santee, CA: Herpetocultural Library, 1997.

Greer, A. E. *The Biology and Evolution of Australian Lizards.* Chipping Norton, New South Wales, Australia: Surrey, Beatty and Sons, Ltd., 1989.

Heatwole, H. F. and J. Taylor. *Australian Ecology Series: Ecology of Reptiles.* Chipping Norton, New South Wales, Australia: Surrey, Beatty and Sons, Ltd., 1987.

Hoser, Raymond. *Australian Reptiles and Frogs.* Mosman, Australia: Pierson Publishing, 1989.

————. *Smuggled: The Underground Trade in Australia's Wildlife.* Sydney, Australia: Apollo Books, 1992.

————. *Smuggled-2. Wildlife Trafficking, Crime and Corruption in Australia.* Doncaster, Victoria, Australia: Kotaki Publishing, 1997.

Lunney, D. and D. Ayers. *Herpetology in Australia: A Diverse Discipline.* Mosman, Australia: Royal Zoological Society of New South Wales, 1993.

Waite, Edgar. *The Reptiles and Amphibians of South Australia,* Facsimile reprint ed. St. Louis: Society for the Study of Amphibians and Reptiles, 1929, reprint edition 1993.

ARTICLES AND PAMPHLETS

Hoser, A. "Pogona—From an Australian Perspective," *Reptilian Magazine* 5, no. 2 (June 1994): 27–41.

Ryback, M. "Vittikin Dragons," *The Vivarium* 7, no. 6 (1994): 6.

Sprackland, R. G. "Australia's Bearded Dragons," *Reptiles Magazine* 1, no. 6 (August 1994): 44–53.

Weis, P. and P. Weis. "Advances in the Breeding and Husbandry of Bearded Dragons," *Reptiles Magazine* 6, no. 4 (April 1998): 10–19.

Weis, P. and P. Weis. "Breeding Bearded Dragons," *Reptiles Magazine* I, no. 4 (August 1994): 54–55.

Wells, R. W. "Hibernation—Bearded Dragons," *Herpetofauna,* 3(1) (1971): 4–6.

Wells, R. W. and C. R. Wellington. "A Synopsis of the Class Reptilia in Australia," *Australian Journal of Herpetology,* 1(3–4): 73–129.

Whitten, G. J. and A. J. Coventry. "Small Pogona vitticeps from the Big Desert, Victoria with notes on other Pogona populations," *Proc. Royal Society of Victoria* 102(2): 117–120.